SAMUEL L. BRENGLE'S HOLY LIFE SERIES

# ANCIENT PROPHETS AND
# MODERN PROBLEMS

Bob Hostetler, General Editor

**wesleyan**
PUBLISHING HOUSE
wphstore.com

CREST BOOKS

Copyright © 2016 by The Salvation Army
Published by Wesleyan Publishing House
Indianapolis, Indiana 46250
Printed in the United States of America
ISBN: 978-1-63257-070-3
ISBN (e-book): 978-1-63257-071-0

Library of Congress Cataloging-in-Publication Data

Brengle, Samuel Logan, 1860-1936.
Ancient prophets and modern problems / Samuel L. Brengle ; Bob Hostetler, general editor.
    pages cm. -- (Samuel L. Brengle's holy life series)
    ISBN 978-1-63257-070-3 (pbk.)
1. Christian life. I. Hostetler, Bob, 1958- editor. II. Title.
    BV4501.3.B7473 2016
    248.4--dc23
                                2015029147

# Contents

# Preface

Samuel Logan Brengle was an influential author, teacher, and preacher on the doctrine of holiness in the late nineteenth to early twentieth century, serving from 1887–1931 as an active officer (minister) in The Salvation Army. In 1889 while he and his wife, Elizabeth Swift Brengle, were serving as corps officers (pastors) in Boston, Massachusetts, a brick thrown by a street "tough" smashed Brengle's head against a door frame and caused an injury severe enough to require more than nineteen months of convalescence. During that treatment and recuperation period, he began writing articles on holiness for The Salvation Army's publication, *The War Cry*, which were later collected and published as a "little red book" under the title *Helps to Holiness*. That book's success led to eight others over the next forty-five years: *Heart Talks on Holiness*, *The Way of Holiness*, *The Soul-Winner's Secret*, *When the Holy Ghost Is Come*, *Love-Slaves*, *Resurrection Life and Power*,

*Ancient Prophets and Modern Problems*, and *The Guest of the Soul* (published in his retirement in 1934).

By the time of his death in 1936, Commissioner Brengle was an internationally renowned preacher and worldwide ambassador of holiness. His influence continues today, perhaps more than any Salvationist in history besides the founders, William and Catherine Booth.

I hope that the revised and updated editions of his books that comprise the Samuel L. Brengle's Holy Life Series will enhance and enlarge that influence, introduce these writings to new readers, and create fresh interest in those who already know the godly wisdom and life-changing power of these volumes.

While I have taken care to preserve the integrity, impact, and voice of the original writing, I have carefully and prayerfully made changes that I hope will facilitate greater understanding and appreciation of Brengle's words for modern readers. These changes include:

- Revising archaic terms (such as the use of King James English) and updating the language to reflect more contemporary usage (such as occasionally employing more inclusive gender references);
- Shortening and simplifying sentence structure and revising punctuation to conform more closely to contemporary practice;
- Explaining specific references of The Salvation Army that will not be familiar to the general population;
- Updating Scripture references (when possible retaining the King James Version—used exclusively in Brengle's writings—but frequently incorporating modern versions, especially when doing so will aid the reader's comprehension and enjoyment);

- Replacing Roman numerals with Arabic numerals and spelled out Scripture references for the sake of those who are less familiar with the Bible;
- Citing Scripture quotes not referenced in the original and noting the sources for quotes, lines from hymns, etc.;
- Aligning all quoted material to the source (Brengle, who often quoted not only Scripture, but also poetry from memory, often quoted loosely in speaking and writing);
- Adding occasional explanatory phrases or endnotes to identify people or events that might not be familiar to modern readers;
- Revising or replacing some chapter titles, and (in *Ancient Prophets and Modern Problems*) moving one chapter to later in the book; and
- Deleting the prefaces that introduced each book and epigraphs that preceded some chapters.

In the preface to Brengle's first book, Commissioner (later General) Bramwell Booth wrote, "This book is intended to help every reader of its pages into the immediate enjoyment of Bible holiness. Its writer is an officer of The Salvation Army who, having a gracious experience of the things whereof he writes, has been signally used of God, both in life and testimony, to the sanctifying of the Lord's people, as well as in the salvation of sinners. I commend him and what he has here written down to every lover of God and His kingdom here on earth."

In the preface to Brengle's last book, *The Guest of the Soul*, The Salvation Army's third general (and successor to Bramwell Booth) wrote: "These choice contributions . . . will, I am sure, serve to strengthen the faith of the readers of this book and impress upon them the joyousness of life when the heart has been opened to the Holy Guest of the Soul."

I hope and pray that this updated version of Brengle's writings will further those aims.

—Bob Hostetler

general editor

# *The Ancient Prophets* 1

For about sixty years I have been reading the Bible, and for nearly fifty I have been reading it through regularly, steadily, and consecutively, year after year. When I have finished Revelation, I turn back to Genesis and begin again. Day by day, I read my chapter or chapters with close and prayerful attention and never without blessing. In this way the Book has become very familiar, but not stale. It is always new, fresh, and illuminating, just as bread and water and sunshine and flowers and birds and mountains and seas and starry heavens are always new and fresh and inspiring.

The sweet stories (and there are no stories so sweet as Bible stories), the sordid stories (and there are none more sordid), the nobilities and brutalities, the saintliness and the sin. The chastity of Joseph (see Gen. 39:6–23), and the shameful, cruel rape by Amnon (see 2 Sam. 13); the drunkenness of Noah (see Gen. 9:21–27), and the sobriety of the

Rechabites (see Jer. 35:2–11); the slaughter of innocent birds and beasts for the sins of men and women, and the slaughter of Canaanites for their own sins (see Deut. 20:16–17). The drunkenness and incest of Lot (see Gen. 19:30–38), and the chaste restraint of Boaz (see Ruth 3); the overthrow of Sodom and Gomorrah (see Gen. 19), and the deliverance of Samaria; the cleansing of Naaman's leprosy, and the smiting of Gehazi with the dreaded disease (see 2 Kings 5); the dastardly wickedness of David followed by his deep penitence as expressed in Psalm 51, and the dog-like fidelity and devotion of Uriah rewarded only by the seduction of his wife and his pitiful murder (see 2 Sam. 11). The duplicity and treachery of Absalom (see 2 Sam. 15), and the devoted love of Jonathan (see 1 Sam. 18, 20); the flaming zeal and despondency and trembling and triumphant finish of Elijah (see 1 Kings 17—2 Kings 2), and the horrid doom and death of Ahab (see 1 Kings 22) and painted, powdered Jezebel (see 2 Kings 9:30–37); the afflictions and dialogues of Job, and his deliverance (see the book of Job); the fall of plotting, rapacious Haman, and the exaltation of Mordecai (see Est. 2–7). The single-eyed devotion of Nehemiah outwitting the wiles of relentless foes, and the treacherous brethren; the swift, sure blow that humbled proud, despotic Nebuchadnezzar (see Dan. 4), and the overthrow and death of drunken Belshazzar (see Dan. 5); the storm, fish, gourd, worm, and blistering sun and hot wind with which God gave kindergarten lessons to bigoted, angry Jonah, and His tender mercy to the little children and cattle of Nineveh (see Jon. 4). The jealousies and envies and contentions of the disciples who each desired to be greatest in the kingdom of Jesus as they, in their carnal childishness, pictured what that kingdom would be (see Luke 22:24–30); the love of Thomas who proposed to go to

Jerusalem and die with Jesus, his stubborn refusal to believe in the resurrection of Jesus unless he could put his fingers into the print of the nails and thrust his hand into Jesus' riven side; the kindly, sure way in which Jesus met the distracted, honest, loving doubter (see John 11:16; 20:24–29); the swearing and lying of Peter and his bitter tears of sorrow (see Luke 22:54–62); the penitent plea of the dying thief on the cross (see Luke 23:32–43); the awful fate of false Ananias and Sapphira (see Acts 5:1–11); the stoning of Stephen (see Acts 7); the conversion of Paul (see Acts 9:1–9); the strange apocalyptic mysteries and imageries of Revelation. All these speak to me in a divine voice with comfort, reproof, correction, admonition, and instruction.

Line upon line, precept upon precept—in picture, parable, story, history, biography, drama, tragedy, poetry, song, and prophecy—I hear God in tender entreaty; in patient instruction; in wise rebuke; in faithful warning; in sweetest promise; in sharp, insistent command; in stern judgment and final sentence, making known to us His mind, His heart, His holiness, His wisdom, His love, and His grace. I see God uplifting the oppressed, the fallen, the lowly, and the penitent and setting them on high and casting down from their thrones and seats of pomp and power the proud, the rich, the arrogant, and the mighty.

My daily reading has again brought me into company with the great prophets—Isaiah, Jeremiah, Ezekiel, Hosea, Micah, Malachi, and others. I live again with them in the midst of the throbbing, tumultuous, teeming life of old Jerusalem, Samaria, Egypt, and Babylon. These prophets are old friends of mine. I have lived with them before, and they have blessed me a thousand times. They have kindled in me some of their flaming zeal for righteousness; their scorn of meanness, duplicity, pride, and worldliness; their jealousy for the living God; their fear for those who forget God and live as though He did not exist; their pity for the ignorant, the erring, the penitent; their anxiety for the future of their people; and their courage in denouncing sin and calling men and women back to the old paths of righteousness.

I stand in awe as I note their intrepidity, their forgetfulness of self in denouncing sin and facing the contempt, the scorn, and then the wrath of princes, priests, and kings. Tradition tells us Isaiah was finally thrust into a hollow log and "sawed in half" (Heb. 11:37 NLT). They counted not their lives dear unto themselves. They were "moved by the Holy Spirit" (2 Pet. 1:21 NLT). They yielded themselves up for service, suffering, or sacrifice as His instruments. They were surrendered and selfless, devoted as soldiers unto death, if necessary, that they might save the nation—and if not the nation, then a remnant who clung to the old paths, who would not bow the knee to Baal, who would not yield to the seductions of fashion and the spirit of the times. They were men and women of the age, but they lived and worked mightily for the ages. They were people of the times, and their message was meant for their times, but it had timeless value because they lived in God and worked for God and spoke only as they were "moved by the Holy Spirit." They were not conformers. They could not be used by ambitious or designing people for partisan purposes.

They were diffident by nature. They shrank from the prophetic office. They did not seek it. It was thrust upon them. God called them, and they went forward under divine constraint.

Listen to Jeremiah's story of his call: "The Lord gave me this message: 'I knew you before I formed you in your mother's womb.

Before you were born I set you apart and appointed you as my prophet to the nations'" (Jer. 1:4–5 NLT).

But Jeremiah shrank from the great task and its fearful responsibility and pleaded: "'O Sovereign LORD . . . I can't speak for you! I'm too young!' The LORD replied, 'Don't say, "I'm too young," for you must go wherever I send you and say whatever I tell you. And don't be afraid of the people, for I will be with you and will protect you'" (Jer. 1:6–8 NLT).

But God did not send Jeremiah forth at his own charges and in his own strength. He never sends forth His prophets like that. He equips them. He humbles them until there is no conceit or strength left in them, like Daniel in Babylon and John on Patmos, and they cry out, as Isaiah did, "Woe is me! For I am lost; for I am a man of unclean lips . . . for my eyes have seen the King, the LORD of hosts!" (Isa. 6:5 ESV), and then He empowers them. And as the Lord touched the lips of Isaiah with living fire, so He touched Jeremiah: "Then the LORD reached out and touched my mouth and said, 'Look, I have put my words in your mouth!'" (Jer. 1:9 NLT). That was his equipment for his great and solemn and dangerous office.

Then the vastness of this man's mission was unfolded to him: "Today I appoint you to stand up against nations and kingdoms"—this lad, who never left the little land of his birth except when dragged down to Egypt against his prophetic protest by murderous, fugitive Jews, now set over the nations and over the kingdoms to root out the rank growth of evil, to "tear down, destroy and overthrow" every high and vicious thing that exalts itself against the knowledge of God, and also to "build up and plant" (Jer. 1:10 NLT). Then God told His prophet: "Get up and prepare for action. Go out and tell them everything I tell you to say. Do not be afraid of them, or I will make you look foolish in front of them" (Jer. 1:17 NLT).

It is a fearful thing to shrink in fear from people and thus fall before the frown of God, but that was the alternative set before this young prophet. Speak boldly and feel the strength of the everlasting arms girding you about, or slink away from the face of mere men and women and be confounded by the Almighty!

It was not a joyous, rose-strewn path the prophets trod. It was perilous, lonely, and blood-stained. Along the way they were ambushed by malignant foes and entrenched monopolies of vested interests and confronted by established custom and the unquestioned practice of kings and princes, priests, and people. The prophet was to set himself in opposition to the nation and the nations. Oh, the loneliness of it! The danger! The thankless task! "For see, today I have made you strong like a fortified city that cannot be captured, like an iron pillar or a bronze wall. You will stand against the whole land—the kings, officials, priests, and people of Judah. They will fight you" (Jer. 1:18–19 NLT).

What a spectacle—a lone man, a child, against the world! "They will fight you, but they will fail. For I am with you, and I will take care of you" (Jer. 1:19 NLT).

Ah, I see! He is not alone. Those who are with him are more than all who are against him. "If God be for us, who can be against us?" (Rom. 8:31 KJV). "The angel of the LORD encamps around those who fear him, and delivers them" (Ps. 34:7 ESV). The prophets were solitary and diffident, but they had access to God. The key to secret resources of exhaustless power and wisdom and grace was given to them. They were equipped with God—God the Holy Spirit. He moved them and they spoke, and their message reverberates through all time, judges all people and nations, and illuminates all history.

Many students of prophecy think the prophets have put into our hands a God-given telescope, through which we can peer into the future and foresee the course of all coming history to the utmost bounds of time, and they prepare elaborate charts and write no end of books and make learned mathematical calculations, and often fix dates for the end of all things. But I have never been helped, but rather confused, in thus trying to interpret the great prophets. Their value to me ever since God sanctified me has consisted not in the light they throw upon generations yet unborn, but the light they throw upon my own generation. I want help to interpret my own times. It is precisely because their messages came from God and are timeless that they are so timely. Their prophecies are meant to enable me to understand the present, to recognize my own duty, to interpret the will and ways of God to the people of my own generation, and to guide the steps of the youth of the next generation to fitness for their solemn, unknown tasks. Beyond that, if I see at all, it is but dimly.

There was an element of foretelling in the prophets' messages, but the infinitely greater element was that of *forth telling*, revealing God Himself—His character, His holiness, His everlasting righteousness that is in eternal, deadly antagonism to all unrighteousness and sin, His benevolence and everlasting love that yearns and woos and waits and seeks the erring and the sinful and forgives the penitent soul—the restoring and redeeming God, who is also a God of judgment, "a consuming fire" (Heb. 12:29 NIV). And it is in the light of this revelation of God's character, nature, mind, heart, will, and ways, that I see my duty and interpret the meaning of my own day, and the problems of my own generation, and am in some measure enabled to forecast the future. And this view of the supreme meaning and value of the prophets for our day seems to me to harmonize with Paul's statement of the great purpose of Scripture: "All Scripture is inspired by God," he wrote, and is useful, not for the gratification of curiosity concerning the distant future but "to teach us what is true and to make us realize what is wrong in our lives. It corrects us when we are wrong and teaches us to do what is right. God uses it to prepare and equip his people to do every good work" (2 Tim. 3:16–17 NLT) in this day and generation.

I fell into a nest of spiritualists once, and the timeliest answer I could make to their pretensions I found in the ancient prophecy of Isaiah and in the words of Jesus. Listen to Isaiah replying to the spiritualists of Jerusalem twenty-five hundred years ago: "Someone may say to you, 'Let's ask the mediums and those who consult the spirits of the dead. With their whisperings and mutterings, they will tell us what to do.' But shouldn't people ask God for guidance? Should the living seek guidance from the dead? Look to God's instructions and teachings! People who contradict his word are completely in the dark" (Isa. 8:19–20 NLT).

And this is matched by the words of Jesus in relating the conversation between Abraham in heaven and the rich man in hell. The rich man wanted Lazarus sent to his brothers on earth to warn them to live in such a way that they would not come to him in hell. "But Abraham said, 'If they won't listen to Moses and the prophets, they won't be persuaded even if someone rises from the dead'" (Luke 16:31 NLT).

My soul is often shocked and shamed by the immodest ways some people dress, but I find that Isaiah was confronted by the same lack of modesty in his day. In Isaiah 3:16–23, he gave a description of the fashions of old Jerusalem that reads as though he had just come from Paris, London, or New York.

There was an entrenched liquor traffic in their day, and those faithful prophets, messengers of God, watchful shepherds of souls, flamed in indignation against the drunkard and the bootlegger:

> What sorrow for those who get up early in the morning looking for a drink of alcohol and spend long evenings drinking wine to make themselves flaming drunk. They furnish wine and lovely music at their grand parties—lyre and harp, tambourine and flute—but they never think about the Lord or notice what he is doing. So my people will go into exile far away because they do not know me.... The grave is licking its lips in anticipation, opening its mouth wide. The great and the lowly and all the drunken mob will be swallowed up. (Isa. 5:11–14 NLT)

The old prophet Habakkuk wrote of the ancient bootlegger, "What sorrow awaits you who make your neighbors drunk! You force your cup on them so you can gloat over their shameful nakedness" (Hab. 2:15 NLT).

Have we problems? Are we confronted by vice and sin in our city? Is evil triumphant and injustice and wickedness entrenched in high places in the state? We shall find light on every problem in the messages of the prophets, and we shall find help and strength in company with them, for they walked with God and lived and spoke and suffered and died for Him. Listen to Habakkuk's prayer: "I have heard all about you, LORD. I am filled with awe by your amazing works. In this time of our deep need, help us again as you did in years gone by . . . remember your mercy" (Hab. 3:2 NLT). His heart was nearly broken by the sin and injustice and wickedness he saw all around him, and he longed for a revival. And then faith in the almightiness, the goodness, of God, and the final triumph of holiness kindled in him, and he shouted out, "For as the waters fill the sea, the earth will be filled with an awareness of the glory of the LORD" (Hab. 2:14 NLT).

And when the cup of the wickedness of the people was full, and the judgment of God fell upon them, and the desolating scourge of the Assyrian invasion swept over the land and left it wasted and bare, he sang: "Even though the fig trees have no blossoms, and there are no grapes on the vines; even though the olive crop fails, and the fields lie empty and barren; even though the flocks die in the fields, and the cattle barns are empty, yet I will rejoice in the LORD! I will be joyful in the God of my salvation!" (Hab. 3:17–18 NLT).

They lived in a day when light was dim. They had no completed Bible. Jesus had not yet come. The cross had not yet been uplifted with its bleeding, redeeming victim. The bars of the tomb had not yet been broken and the iron doors of death had not swung open that the light of the resurrection might stream through. Pentecost had not yet come. But they believed in the "mighty God, the everlasting Father." They believed Him to be the "Prince of Peace" and that upon His shoulders rested all government, and that "of his government and peace there shall be no end" (Isa. 9:6–7 KJV). They believed that however high sin might vault it would be cast down, it would not finally triumph—that however deeply entrenched and strongly garrisoned injustice and arrogance and pride might be, yet they would be rooted out, pulled down, and trampled in the dust.

But though they flamed like fire heated sevenfold against sin, they had hearts as tender as tiny children, and they wept for sinful and struggling souls, and breathed out promises as gentle as light falling on the eyes of sleeping babes. It was God, the Holy One, in these devoted, yielded prophets that flamed against iniquity, that sobbed and wept over the desolations sin wrought, and that gave promises that still fall into our hearts with heaven's own benediction.

Oh Jeremiah, my brother and friend in this ministry of judgment and mercy, this proclamation of the "goodness and severity of God" (Rom. 11:22 KJV), how I thank you, and thank God for you, as across centuries and millennia you still whisper into my listening ears and my longing heart those sweet words: "The LORD has appeared of old to me, saying: 'Yes, I have loved you with an everlasting love; therefore with lovingkindness I have drawn you'" (Jer. 31:3 NKJV).

I am a lonely man, and yet I am not lonely. With my open Bible, I live with prophets, priests, and kings; I walk and hold communion with apostles, saints, and martyrs, and with Jesus, and my eyes see the King in His beauty and the land that is far off.

# *Why I Wanted My Wife to Be My Wife*

It was my pleasant privilege once to be entertained for several days in the home of some Swedish friends. The family consisted of a husband and wife and three exceptionally bright and lovely children. He was a strong, manly fellow who had made his way to the front rank in his chosen work by sheer force of character, industry, and ability. She was a happy wife who did her own housework, rejoiced in her husband's success, and mothered the children with wise and loving care.

One morning at breakfast, she told me (in the most charming broken English) the one test by which she decided the fate of several suitors, and by which she was assured that in her husband she had at last met her heart's mate with whom she could gladly and unfalteringly link her life for better or worse till death.

During her childhood in her old-fashioned, economical Swedish home, she had to darn stockings and socks, something she disliked very much to do, but which unwittingly was developing in her a selective instinct that was finally to bring her great joy. When she had grown into the radiant beauty of young womanhood and young men began to pay her attention, each appeared as a prospective husband. And to each she applied this test: "Would I be willing to darn his socks?" In each instance, there was a revulsion of feeling that settled the fate of the young man, until she met the one who was to be her husband.

When she applied the test to him, her heart leaped with joy at the prospect. She felt she would gladly spend her life darning his socks, and she longed to begin at once on whole bureau drawers full of them. She did not tell—and possibly she could not tell—what it was in him that made him different from all others. But something in his presence or person unlocked a treasure-store of love and sacrificial devotion in her heart that made her sure that of all men he was the one to whom she could commit herself without doubt or fear. It was what she discovered in herself quite as much as what she found in him that made her certain.

When Abraham Lincoln made his call for volunteers in the War between the States, my youthful father heard and responded to the call. He left his young wife and baby boy and went off to the war, and at the Siege of Vicksburg paid the last full tribute of devotion to his country, while the young widowed mother wept and the little boy looked on with wide-eyed and uncomprehending wonder. He had been an ideal husband and for three years had made Mother supremely happy. Never once did he speak a cross word or show to her other than the most tender and chivalrous devotion. The memory of his love was always with her, and as I grew she would hug me to her heart and tell me how happy my father had made her, and then she would add, as she looked me straight in the eyes, "And someday my boy will make some woman unspeakably happy."

So naturally I came to feel that was part of the mission of my life, one of the objects of my being, to make some woman happy—while to injure a woman, to mar her life and blast her happiness, seemed to me (and still seems) the most supreme cursedness and treason against the most sacred rights and claims of humanity.

From Mother I unconsciously got a high ideal of gentle sweetness and purity, and all womanly virtues that adorn a home and make it a haven of rest and a center of inspiration, courage, and noble ambition. Then one day at school word came to me: "Quick! Come home; Mother is dying!"

When I got home, Mother was dead. The love light had fled from her beautiful eyes, but a smile was on her sweet face. They buried her, but her spirit was with me and the memory of her sweet, womanly character was enshrined deep in my heart. And in all my boyish loves and dreams, it was sweetness and purity rather than flashing beauty and wit that kindled tender emotions within me. My wife must be gentle and sweet and pure of heart. This I gathered unconsciously from my mother.

Following Mother's death, I prepared for college and spent four years in a university in the Midwest. What a bevy of lovely girls surrounded me there! We frolicked and flirted and picnicked and were as frank and open and wholesome in our relations with each other as brothers and sisters, but my heart was lost to none of them. Two of them were as beautiful as any picture John Singer Sargent ever painted, but they were frivolous. One had the most wondrous eyes and the most perfect complexion I ever saw, with masses of lovely hair and a form that would have graced a ducal palace; she was intellectual, also, but it was Lady Clare Vere de Vere[1] transplanted to the Ohio Valley:

> Faultily faultless, icily regular, splendidly null,
> Dead perfection, no more.[2]

Another was very charming, but she lacked depth of character, I thought, and was too petite. Yet another was rich in character, one of the best students I ever knew, and one of the finest of women, but stiff in manner, and there was an irregularity about her features that I regretted (in the callow years of young manhood, very small defects—which may not be defects at all and would probably be unnoticed by older and wiser men—may cause Cupid's darts to miss the mark).

My intellectual awakening was slow, and I do not think those four years quite completed the process, but I was sufficiently awakened to see and feel that my wife must have a range of vision and thought beyond the neighborhood in which we might live, or I could not be happy with her. She must be educated, know books, have some knowledge of the world's best thought, and the culture that only this can give.

I was not myself deeply religious, though I was a member of the church, taught in the Sunday school, sang in the choir, and worked in the college YMCA, but I missed in all those lovely girls a religious conviction and influence which I now see I needed and craved and would have heartily welcomed from any one of them.

Young men may appear careless concerning religious matters, but I am persuaded from a rather wide acquaintance and experience that they do not resent but respond promptly (though maybe jauntily at first or silently for a time) to the gentle spiritual touch of the young woman who has vital spiritual knowledge and is frank and natural and modestly courageous in the expression of her convictions, who appeals to everything that is best in them and shames everything that is false and morally wrong. In these things, young men are often more willing to be led than to take the lead, and here, if they would, young women could often gain a commanding and gracious and lifelong influence over young men, an influence which would be welcomed as guiding, restraining, inspiring, and greatly longed for and needed in the midst of fierce temptations to which young men are subject.

It was while continuing my professional studies at an Eastern university that the conviction possessed me that my wife must not only have sweet womanly virtues and be adorned with refinement and the culture of the schools, but also that she must be genuinely religious—must love God and His law supremely—for without this, I realized, we would fail in the highest fellowship. With this love and loyalty to God abounding, I knew that her love and loyalty to me could not fail.

Indeed, I came not through any experience but through awakened spiritual insight to distrust the permanency of a human love that is not replenished and enriched by the overflow of a divine love, and a loyalty that is not purified and reinforced by the reverential fear and love of God. Where this fear and love abide there can be no failure. "Many waters cannot quench love" (Song 8:7 KJV) that is kindled and fed from this central and exhaustless fire.

But where could I find such a woman? Solomon was a very wise man and had a wide marital experience, and he said, "A prudent wife is from the LORD" (Prov. 19:14 KJV). If she is from the Lord, why not ask Him for her? Why not pray to Him to find her? And this I did.

Marriage is a divine institution, is surrounded by divine sanctions, and should be entered into with a sense of its divine character and responsibilities and blessings, which, abused, can turn into the most fateful of curses. Therefore, God's blessing and guidance should be sought in every step that leads to it.

The year I went east to study, three girls from one of the leading women's colleges of America went abroad to see Europe, and in London, to their utter surprise and joy, they found the Lord in The Salvation Army.

One of them He had chosen for me.

To her heart of sweet womanly graces, and to her culture, He added His grace and spirit. Two years later we met, and I fell in love—I lost my heart. Here she was—the sweet, gracious, cultured woman, filled with God's love, one my head and my heart approved, and for whose dear sake I had denied myself in lonely hours of fierce temptation, though I had not seen her face, and for whom I had prayed and watched and waited.

At an appropriate time, not then being able to see her, I wrote and told her all, and she sent me the sweetest letter—and the bitterest—I ever received. She said she wept at the pain it must give me, and she felt that my love and union with me would put the crown upon her womanhood, but there were obstacles in the way—obstacles she feared were insuperable. She then generously mentioned two others, with either of whom she thought I might be happier than with her. At her invitation I met them, and they were lovely women, but to my mind they were "as water unto wine,"[3] and I pressed my suit in spite of obstacles.

One day she gave me an anonymous little book. I read it with the deepest interest and emotion, not once suspecting who had written it, and when I learned it was her book I loved her none the less.

On another day we were driving among the beautiful hills around her home, and some occasion arose that led her to tell me of a nameless baby, a little child of lawless passions and the night, whose tender life was wasting away through the ignorance and lack of care on the part of its young mother. She coaxed the mother to let her have the baby for a while and took it home and kept it for months, nursing it back to rosy health and dimpled sweetness. And as she talked about that baby I felt that in her heart were the germs of the richest and tenderest mother love, and for this I loved her all the more, for I felt that if I ever had a wife, I wanted one who would not shun but welcome motherhood with great and solemn joy.

On yet another day we stood by the piano in her father's home, when suddenly she turned, slipped out into the hall, and left me. My eyes followed her and my whole heart went out after her.

I did not want to die for her, but to live for her. I wanted to put my arms around her, comfort her, provide for her, protect her, bear her burdens, be her shield, and receive every blow of adversity or sorrow or misfortune that might befall her. I no longer thought of what she might bring or give to me, but only of what I might give to and suffer for her.

And then and there, at last, I had found and entered the pure world of sacrificial love and utter devotion reached by the wife of my Swedish friend—the only world in which I could fulfill my mother's prophecy.

The key that will open a Yale lock was made for the lock, and the woman who can open the inmost treasure-store of a man's heart and can bring forth the refined gold of unselfish love, was made for that man. By this I knew that she, who for twenty-eight wonderful and blessed years was my wife, and became the happy mother of my children, was God's woman for me. And that is why I wanted my wife to be my wife!

### NOTES

1. A reference to a poem by Alfred Lord Tennyson about an aristocratic lady who flirted with lower-class men only to reject them once they were interested.

2. Alfred Lord Tennyson, "Maud," pt. 1, section 2, lines 82–83, public domain.

3. Alfred Lord Tennyson, "Locksley Hall," 1835, public domain.

# The Cost of Winning Souls 3.

Some years ago a young Salvation Army officer (minister) wrote to her superior saying she meant to resign if she could not get souls saved. But she did not resign.

A pastor who was famous for the revivals that swept his churches and moved the communities where he labored was sent to a big church in New York City. As he walked into a gathering of ministers, he heard them whispering among themselves, "He will find New York different. It is the graveyard of revival reputations." Right there he resolved and publicly declared that there would be a revival in his church or there would be a funeral in his parsonage.

Little faith sees the difficulties and often accepts defeat without a fight. Great faith sees God and fights against all odds and—even if the Enemy apparently triumphs—wins moral and spiritual victory, as did Christ on Calvary and as did the martyrs who perished in flame. What could be more complete to doubting hearts and the eyes of unbelief than the defeat of Christ on the cross or of Thomas Cranmer and Nicholas Ridley in the fire! And yet it was then that their victory over the Enemy was supreme. The Spirit of Jesus is the spirit of conquest. When Paul—filled with passionate love for Christ, whom he had persecuted, and burning with eager desire to see others experience the great salvation that had reached him—went forth to evangelize the Roman Empire, enemies confronted and hunted him with the same deadly hate and murderous opposition he had once shown to the Jerusalem Christians, while every city he entered reeked with unmentionable vices and reveled in licentious idolatries. He had no completed Bible, no religious press, no missionary organization behind him to ensure his support, and the very name of Christ was unknown, while Caesar was honored as a god.

The wealth, learning, philosophy, political power, religions, vested interests of the world, and the age-long habits, passions, and inflamed appetites of humanity were all opposed to him. Don Quixote's valorous attack on windmills did not appear more absurd than Paul's assault on the sin, corruption, and entrenched evils of the world of his day. And he wielded no other weapon than his personal testimony and the story of a crucified, resurrected Jewish peasant carpenter, whom he heralded as the Son of God and the Savior and Judge of the world, before whom everyone—from the emperor to the lowest slave—must someday appear to be judged for their deeds and be rewarded with eternal bliss or doomed to endless shame and woe. Paul died, but he won souls.

Immeasurable difficulties faced John and Charles Wesley when they and George Whitefield began their careers that reawakened

Christendom. The clergy were (as a class) utterly unspiritual, given over to drinking, horse racing, and fox hunting with the gentry. The educated classes were, in large measure, skeptical and licentious, while the lower classes in the cities were only too often debased and drunken, and found their pleasures in cockfighting and racing dogs on Sundays. But in the midst of these desolate and desperate conditions, the Wesleys started the greatest revival since the apostolic age, and snatched souls by the myriads from the very jaws of hell.

And amid conditions almost, if not equally, as dark and forbidding, the founder of The Salvation Army began and carried on his work that has directly touched and won millions of souls and an even larger number indirectly, quickening the faith and lifting the spiritual level of the whole Christian world, and touching with soul-saving power and life-giving hope great populations in many lands.

But none of these world-embracing, epoch-making revivals began in a large way. Paul usually made an address and gave his testimony in a synagogue—a small meeting-place of the Jews—until he was excluded, and then he went to some home or room that was opened to him. This was followed by house-to-house visitation, often after a day's work at tent-making. The Wesleys began in a similarly humble way, and so did William Booth.

Great revivals among God's people and awakenings among the ungodly never begin in a great way. They begin as oak trees begin. There is nothing startling and spectacular about the beginning of an oak tree. In darkness, in loneliness, an acorn gives up its life. And the oak, at first only a tiny root and a tiny stem of green, is born out of the dissolution and death of the acorn. So revivals are born, so souls are won, and so the kingdom of God comes. Someone no longer trying to save him- or herself or advance his or her own interests dies—dies to self; to the world; to the praise of others; to the ambition for promotion, place, or power—and lives unto Christ, lives to save others, and the awakening comes. Souls are born into the kingdom of God, and they rally round their leader and in turn become soul-winners. Jesus said, "Unless a kernel of wheat falls to the ground and dies, it remains only a single seed. But if it dies, it produces many seeds" (John 12:24 NIV). And so He "endured the cross, despising the shame" (Heb. 12:2 KJV), and died that He might win souls, save men and women, and bring "many sons and daughters to glory" (Heb. 2:10 NIV).

"Anyone who wants to serve me must follow me," said Jesus (John 12:26 NLT). In other words, they must lose their old lives, their old ambitions, their old estimate of values for His sake, His cause, and the souls they would win and for whom He died. "Those who love their life in this world will lose it. Those who care nothing for their life in this world will keep it for eternity" (John 12:25 NLT).

That is the way to become a soul-winner; that is the price that must be paid. The Master could find no easier way, and He can show no easier way to us. It is costly. But shall we wish to win eternal and infinite values cheaply? "For the joy that was set before him [He] endured the cross" (Heb. 12:2 KJV). What joy? The joy of having the Father's approval and of saving souls from eternal death and of "bringing many sons and daughters to glory" (Heb. 2:10 NIV). Shall we hope to share that joy by some cheap service that calls for no uttermost devotion, no whole burnt offering, no final and complete sacrifice? Not otherwise has anyone ever become a soul-winner. We may move upon the surface of people's lives, we may touch their emotions, we may lead them to easy, nonsacrificial religious exercises and activities and think we are saving souls, but we do not really win them until we constrain them to follow us, as we follow Christ, through death—death to sin, death to the flesh and the world—into newness of life unto holiness.

This was Paul's way. "And now I am bound by the Spirit to go to Jerusalem. I don't know what awaits me, except that the Holy Spirit tells me in city after city that jail and suffering lie ahead. But my life is worth nothing to me unless I use it for finishing the work assigned me by the Lord Jesus—the work of telling others the Good News about the wonderful grace of God" (Acts 20:22–24 NLT). It was not easy for Paul. He counted the cost. He paid the price. He turned neither to the right hand nor the left. He marched straight forward.

He was commissioned "to open [people's] eyes, and to turn them from darkness to light, and from the power of Satan unto God, that they may receive forgiveness of sins, and inheritance among them which are sanctified by faith" in Christ (Acts 26:18 KJV). And he added, "I was not disobedient unto the heavenly vision" (Acts 26:19 KJV). "Whatever gain I had, I counted as loss for the sake of Christ. Indeed, I count everything as loss because of the surpassing worth of knowing Christ Jesus my Lord. For his sake I have suffered the loss of all things and count them as rubbish, in order that I may gain Christ" (Phil. 3:7–8 ESV).

It is as we thus count all things as loss and so win Christ that we are empowered to win souls. This is the standard we must set for ourselves, and to which we must woo and draw our younger colleagues by the compulsion of love and faithful teaching and example.

The psalmist David, in his penitential prayer, cried to God for a clean heart and a right spirit, for the joy of salvation, and the enabling of the Holy Spirit. "Then," he said, "I will teach transgressors your ways, and sinners will return to you" (Ps. 51:13 ESV). David felt that if he would effectively teach and convert others his heart must be pure, his spirit must be right. So then the cost of winning souls includes the price that must be paid for a pure heart. I must be clean, my spirit must be right, I must hold back no part of the price, I must bring all the tithes into God's storehouse, if I would be a soul-winner.

"He who is wise wins souls," wrote Solomon (Prov. 11:30 NASB). Then, if I would be a soul-winner, I must pay the price of wisdom. Wisdom cannot be bought with silver and gold. It cannot be passed on like an inheritance from parent to child. It cannot be learned, as we learn mathematics or the sciences, in schools and colleges. It comes only through experience in following Christ.

> Knowledge comes, but wisdom lingers, and he bears a laden breast,
>
> Full of sad experience, moving toward the stillness of his rest.[1]

He or she who wants wisdom must not shrink from suffering. "When reviled, we bless; when persecuted, we endure; when slandered, we entreat," wrote Paul (1 Cor. 4:12–13 ESV). Suffering did not daunt him. Abuse and neglect did not embitter him. When his converts were turned against him, he wrote, "I will not be burdensome to you: for I seek not yours but you. . . . And I will very gladly spend and be spent for you; though the more abundantly I love you, the less I be loved. . . . We do all things, dearly beloved, for your edifying" (2 Cor. 12:14–15, 19 KJV).

Anyone with that spirit is full of wisdom, the wisdom of God, "the wisdom that is from above," which is "first pure, then peaceable, gentle, and easy to be intreated, full of mercy and good fruits, without partiality, and without hypocrisy" (James 3:17 KJV). And such people win souls. Their lives, their example, their spirit, their speech are compelling, and they win and knit others to Christ.

The soul-winner must not despise the day of small things. It is better to speak to a small company and win a half-dozen of them to the Savior than to speak to a thousand and have no one saved or sanctified, though they all go away lauding the leader and exclaiming, "Wasn't that grand!"

Some years ago I went to a large city where The Salvation Army owned an auditorium seating nearly a thousand people, and where I thought we had a flourishing corps (church). The officer couple in charge had unusual ability, but had become stale and spiritually lifeless. Where hundreds should have greeted me, fifty tired, listless people were present, twenty of whom were unkempt children. When I rose to lead the singing, there were three songbooks among us, one of which was mine. The officer ran off downstairs to pick up a few more books, and while we waited I was fiercely tempted to walk off the platform and leave the place, telling him I would not spend my strength helping someone with no more spirit and interest than he manifested. Then I looked at the people before me—tired miners, poor and wearied wives, and little, unshepherded children, peering at me with dull, quizzical eyes as though wondering whether I would club them or feed them, give them stones or bread for their hunger—and my heart was swept with a great wave of pity for them, these sheep without a shepherd. So I set myself with full purpose of heart to bless and feed and save them, and in the next six days that big auditorium was crowded and we rejoiced over ninety souls seeking the Savior. True soul-winners count not their lives dear. They give themselves desperately to their task, and there are times when, as Knox prayed, "Give me Scotland, or I die," so they sob and cry, "Give me souls, or I die."

That New York pastor I mentioned earlier had a revival in his church. There was no funeral in the parsonage. Day and night he cried to God for souls. Every afternoon he visited the people in their homes, offices, and shops. He climbed so many stairways that he said if they had been piled one on the other they would have taken him well up toward the moon. For a month or more, he devoted his mornings to study of the Bible and to reading the biographies of soul-winners, books on revivals, revival lectures and sermons, revival songs, and revival stories and anecdotes. He saturated his mind and heart with the very spirit of revivals. He looked into the grave, into hell, into heaven. He studied Calvary. He meditated on eternity. He stirred up his pity and compassion for the people. He cried to God for the Holy Spirit and for power, faith, wisdom, fervor, joy, and love. He woke up in the night and prayed and planned his strategy. He enlisted such members of his church as were spiritual to help him. When he won someone for Christ he enlisted that person as a helper in the fight. And God swept the church with revival fire. Hundreds were won to Christ. Oh, how unfailing is God. However present and ready to help is the Holy Spirit! How surely is Jesus present where men and women gather in His name!

That young Salvation Army officer to whom I referred did not resign. One night, as she closed the meeting, she asked the soldiers (church members) to remain with her for a short while. Then she opened her heart to them. She told them of the letter she had written. She said she could not continue in the work unless she could see souls saved. Many drunkards were in the city. Their homes were being ruined, their wives neglected, and they were hastening to hell because of the drink. She asked her soldiers to remain and spend an hour in prayer with her and for her, and for the salvation of souls, especially of the drunkards of the city. They stayed, and for an hour they prayed. God heard and drew nigh, and Jesus was in their midst.

After the next public meeting, she again requested the soldiers to remain, and again they prayed for an hour or more, and Jesus was there. And after every public meeting for a week or ten days or more, they stayed and prayed, and Jesus was in their midst. And then one night, somewhat to their surprise—strange that we should be surprised at answered prayer—the worst drunkard in the city, with several of his pals, came to the meeting and experienced new life in Christ. Next, his whole family was won, and they all became soldiers. In a brief time twelve drunkards came to faith, and that woman had a blessed revival on her hands. And not only did lost souls enter the kingdom of God but a sincere woman's ministry was saved as well.

We may be sweet singers, eloquent and moving preachers, skillful organizers, masters of crowds, wizards of finance, or popular and commanding leaders; but if we are not soul-winners, if we do not make men and women see the meaning and winsomeness of Jesus, hunger for His righteousness and purity, and bow to Him in full loyalty, then we lack the "one thing . . . needful" (Luke 10:42 KJV). And yet that one thing is within the reach of us all if we live for it, if we put it first, if we shrink not from the cost. We may be, we should be, we shall be at all cost winners of souls!

## NOTE

1. Alfred Lord Tennyson, "Locksley Hall," 1835, public domain.

# *As with Sons* 4

The author of the book of Hebrews wrote, "Bear hardship for the sake of discipline. God is treating you like sons and daughters! What child isn't disciplined by his or her father? But if you don't experience discipline, which happens to all children, then you are illegitimate and not real sons and daughters" (Heb. 12:7–8 CEB).

If I turn to the commentaries of Matthew Henry; Adam Clark; Jamieson, Fawcett, and Brown; or others, I would probably find some wise and useful comments about those verses. But life itself will furnish the best and most instructive comment to men or women with open eyes, who observe, meditate, think, and remember the chastenings of their own youth.

For some days, I have been an amused and deeply interested observer of the chastening or discipline of one of my little grandsons who is not yet a year old. He is almost bursting with pep. He simply bubbles over with life. One of his chief joys is to get into his bath. It is perfectly delicious to watch him as he kicks and coos and gurgles and splashes water all over himself and anyone who comes near, blinks when water pops into his eyes, and revels in one of the chief joys of his young life. But how he loathes being undressed and redressed before and after his bath! He kicks and flourishes his arms in impatient protest, cries and objects in all manner of baby ways, while his insistent mother ignores all his objections, not asking what he likes but putting on him such clothes as she thinks best, plumps him into his baby carriage, and wheels the rosy little rogue out onto the porch for his morning nap in the sunshine and soft spring winds.

All this to him is chastening, discipline, and training. It is not severe but gentle and wise, though to him much of it is painful. "For the moment all discipline seems painful rather than pleasant, but later"—let us note this "but later" and give thanks and be humble—"it yields the peaceful fruit of righteousness to those who have been trained by it" (Heb. 12:11 ESV). The child will learn slowly, but surely, through this unwavering process that he must submit to rightful authority and superior wisdom, and that those things that are right and good must come first, not only those things that are pleasant at present. Then someday he will discover that all this painful insistence of his unyielding mother was the expression of wise, thoughtful, sacrificial love.

If his father and mother are wise, their chastening, or discipline, will grow with the growth and unfold with the unfolding of this baby boy. They will probably often find themselves sorely perplexed, their hearts will be searched, and they will discover that their own minds and spirits are being disciplined, chastened, in ways that to them are for the present "painful." But if they are humble and prayerful and patient and trustful, and always put the right and the good first, they will find that while they discipline the child, God in love is training them, and bringing them into intimate, understanding fellowship with Himself in His great and sore travail to save and train a fallen race that wants its own way and prefers pleasure to righteousness. And, if they are wise, they will note that God is just as insistent in disciplining them as they are in disciplining their baby boy, and for the same reason—for their good. "God is treating you like sons and daughters" (Heb. 12:7 CEB).

As the baby gets older, the discipline at times may have to be sterner and more severe. If he will yield to his parents' word, he will be happy. But if he will not be guided by word, then it may be necessary to use the rod. "The rod and reproof give wisdom," wrote Solomon, "but a child left to himself brings shame to his mother" (Prov. 29:15 ESV). I do not know that I can improve upon Solomon; he mentions the rod before reproof, but I would suggest reproof before the rod. Gentle measures should be used first. The Lord pleads with His people. "Do not be like a senseless horse or mule that needs a bit and bridle to keep it under control" (Ps. 32:9 NLT). He has a better, gentler way: "I will instruct you and teach you in the way you should go; I will guide you with My eye" (Ps. 32:8 NKJV). How tender and gracious God is! And how often I have seen a wise mother counsel and guide her child with her eye.

But the child that will not be so guided should be taught by sterner ways. It is not true love that withholds proper discipline from the child. "Those who spare the rod of discipline hate their children. Those who love their children care enough to discipline them" (Prov. 13:24 NLT).

Let us learn from the heavenly Father how to be true fathers and mothers:

- "Discipline your children while there is hope. Otherwise you will ruin their lives" (Prov. 19:18 NLT).
- "Discipline your children, and they will give you peace of mind and will make your heart glad" (Prov. 29:17 NLT).
- "A youngster's heart is filled with foolishness, but physical discipline will drive it far away" (Prov. 22:15 NLT).

The parent who has exercised the kindest, wisest, yet firmest and most unvarying control of the child eventually receives the highest and deepest affection of the child. But firmness must be balanced by justice or the child will be embittered and made into a sullen rebel.

My sweet mother was kind, but she was not invariably firm. After my father's death, she was left alone with me, her tiny boy. All the wellsprings of her deep love and tender affection flowed around me, and often when she should have been firm and unbending, she yielded to melting tenderness, of which I was quick to take advantage. I do not remember it, but she herself told me that I would have been spoiled had she not married again and found in my stepfather a counterpoise to her tenderness. He was firm and unbending, and I stood in awe of him, much to my profit. He had a boy near my own age, and he meted out discipline between us in even measure. But while he was firm with us, I felt in my boy heart that he was not always just. He was hasty. He would fly into a passion. He was not patient and did not always take time to find out all the facts, and at times I was embittered, and might have been spoiled by him as surely as by mother's fondness had their methods not in a measure balanced each other. They both needed a finer, firmer self-control to wisely discipline growing boys.

My sweet, lovely mother needed to firmly control the tenderness of her feelings and the floods of her affection, while my stepfather needed to control the unthinking quickness of his snap judgments and the nervous and passionate haste of his explosive temper. But while he punished us boys sometimes when we did not deserve it, yet he missed us sometimes when we did, so betwixt and between we got about what we deserved, on the whole. I have no quarrel in my memory with his dealings, but only gratitude and affection and a deep wish that in some way after all these scores of years I could repay the debt I owe him.

But it is to my darling mother I owe my deepest debt of love and gratitude. As I grew older, her gentleness and tenderness became the most powerful instrument of discipline to my wayward spirit, just as grace is mightier to break and refashion hard hearts than law, and Mount Calvary more influential for redemption than Mount Sinai. Can eternity blot out the memory and remove the ache in my heart caused by a look she gave me when I was but a lad of thirteen years? My stepfather had been unfair (I felt) in a demand upon me one day, and I flamed inwardly with resentment. When my mother and a lady friend appeared, all my pent-up wrath exploded in hot, angry words about my stepfather. Mother tried to get me to be silent but I was too angry. I blurted out all that was in my heart. I had my say. But that night, as I went to kiss Mother goodnight, as I always did, she gave me a look of grief and pain that has stayed with me for more than half a century. Her loved form has moldered beneath green grass and daisies, the rain has beaten upon her grave, and snows of over half a hundred winters have shrouded it in their mantling whiteness, but the chastening pain that entered my heart from her wounded heart with that look is with me still. To this day, after all these years, I can shut my eyes at any time and see the pained, grieved look in the lovely eyes of my dear mother.

If parents have trained their children so wisely as to hold their deep affection while commanding their highest respect, there will come a time when a look will be weightier than law, and the character of the loved and esteemed parent will exert a greater authority to mold and fashion the child in righteousness than anything the parent can say or do. The commanding authority and chastenings of law must yield to the more penetrating and purifying self-discipline imposed by the recognized faith and hope and love of the parent, and disappointing that parent will bring the deepest and most abiding pain to the child's own heart. This is God's way.

There was a time when Jesus turned and rebuked Peter with sharp, incisive words: "Get behind me, Satan! For you are not setting your mind on the things of God, but on the things of man" (Mark 8:33 ESV). But eventually Jesus' character and spirit had so far mastered Peter that a look sufficed to break his heart. Peter in a panic of fear denied Jesus, cursed and swore, "'Man, I don't know what you are talking about.' And immediately, while he was still speaking, the rooster crowed." And Jesus "turned and looked at Peter." That was all, but it was sufficient. "Peter left the courtyard, weeping bitterly" (Luke 22:60–62 NLT). I think never till his dying day could Peter forget that look. It broke his heart, and "the sacrifices of God are a broken spirit . . . and contrite heart" (Ps. 51:17 ESV).

This is the final triumph of all the chastenings of God's love. Once He has thus broken us He can henceforth guide us with His eye. We shall be happy when we come to look upon the perplexing, painful, and harassing things of life—as well as the plain and pleasant things—as instruments in the hands of our heavenly Father for the chastening, polishing, and perfecting of our character and the widening of our influence.

John Bunyan's enemies offered to release him from prison if he would preach no more, but he replied that he would let moss grow over his eyes before he would make such a promise, so they kept him in that filthy Bedford jail among the vilest criminals for twelve weary years. They thought to stop his ministry, but they only made his ministry age-long and worldwide, for during those years he meditated, dreamed, rejoiced, and wrote his undying book, *The Pilgrim's Progress*. The limitation imposed upon him in prison was God's opportunity to liberate his mental and spiritual powers.

Paul would have been lost and unknown to us in the dimness of antiquity, if it were not for his letters written from prison. Nero put him in chains and shut his body up in a dungeon, and through this limitation God liberated Paul's influence for all time and for the whole human race. It is a law that liberation comes by limitation. We die to live. We are buried to be resurrected. We are chastened to be perfected.

"O the depth of the riches both of the wisdom and knowledge of God! How unsearchable are his judgments, and his ways past finding out!" (Rom. 11:33 KJV).

# The Seamless Robe of Jesus 5

Jesus never pitied Himself, nor did He seek the pity of anyone else. One day He asked His disciples, "Who do people say that the Son of Man is?" (Matt. 16:13 NLT).

"John the Baptist," replied one.

"Elijah," said another.

"Jeremiah or one of the prophets," answered a third.

"But who do you say I am?" He asked.

"You are the Messiah, the Son of the living God," replied ever-ready Simon Peter (Matt. 16:16 NLT).

At last their eyes had pierced through the veil of His humanity, the disguise of His lowly village ancestry and His humble occupation as a carpenter, and recognized the King, King Eternal, King of Kings, and Lord of Lords. The splendor of His being, before which seraphim and cherubim, angels and archangels veil their faces, was so accommodated to their poor eyes and minds that their eyes were not blinded and they were not afraid.

"Jesus replied, 'You are blessed, Simon son of John, because my Father in heaven has revealed this to you. You did not learn this from any human being'" (Matt. 16:17 NLT).

The secret was out! The Son of God, the Eternal Word, "full of grace and truth" (John 1:14 KJV), was made flesh and was in the world, dwelling among humankind. But the secret must not go further just yet, so He "sternly warned the disciples not to tell anyone that he was the Messiah" (Matt. 16:20 NLT). It must not be spread abroad. He must draw the veil yet closer about Himself, that only sincere, humble souls might know Him, that the sin of humanity might run its course, and its malignity and utter enmity to God might be revealed in their treatment of Him, the well-beloved, only begotten Son of the Father.

"From then on Jesus began to tell his disciples plainly that it was necessary for him to go to Jerusalem, and that he would suffer many terrible things at the hands of the elders, the leading priests, and the teachers of religious law. He would be killed, but on the third day he would be raised from the dead" (Matt. 16:21 NLT).

Such statements, it should seem, would have dumbfounded the disciples. But not Peter; his poor, dull mind was roused and his tongue loosed, and he took Jesus aside "and began to reprimand him for saying such things. 'Heaven forbid, Lord,' he said. 'This will never happen to you!'" (Matt. 16:22 NLT).

The marginal reading of Peter's wording is, "Pity yourself!" But Jesus did not pity Himself, and He would have none of Peter's pity nor worldly counsel and comfort. He said, "Get away from me, Satan!

You are a dangerous trap to me. You are seeing things merely from a human point of view, not from God's" (Matt. 16:23 NLT).

But while Jesus would not pity Himself, nor even permit Peter to counsel pity, what could be more pathetic, humanly speaking, than the scene at the cross, when He—the most loving and devoted of the sons of men, and the poorest—was stripped of His only suit of clothes, His only earthly possession, and nailed nude to the cross to die, while those who crucified Him divided the poor little bundle of clothes among themselves and cast lots for His seamless robe? His robe without seam, that must not be torn. Think of that careless, cruel soldier stalking about in the robe of Jesus. What a picture!

But while the soldiers, for their own selfish purposes, spared the seamless robe that day, how often has it been torn since then, and that by those who profess to know and love Him.

I like to think of that first society of His people, which we now speak of as the early church, as the seamless robe of Jesus. It enshrined His spiritual presence. He clothed Himself with it as with a garment. Through its members He, the risen Christ, was still seen by human eyes.

He was revealed in its spiritual life. To the wonder-struck multitude on the day of Pentecost, amazed at the glowing, fire-baptized disciples, and inquiring, "What can this mean?" (Acts 2:12 NLT) and the others who, mocking, said, "They're just drunk" (Acts 2:13 NLT)—Peter replied, "God raised Jesus from the dead, and we are all witnesses of this. Now he is exalted to the place of highest honor in heaven, at God's right hand. And the Father, as he had promised, gave him the Holy Spirit to pour out upon us, just as you see and hear today" (Acts 2:32–33 NLT).

The radiant, joy-filled, fearless, conquering life of the early church was the life, the presence of Christ, in its members. "It is no longer I who live, but Christ lives in me," wrote Paul (Gal. 2:20 NLT). And "When Christ who is our life appears, then you also will appear with Him in glory" (Col. 3:4 NKJV).

He was made manifest in the activities of the early church. After healing the lame man at the temple gate called Beautiful, Peter asked the Jerusalem crowd, "People of Israel . . . what is so surprising about this? And why stare at us as though we had made this man walk by our own power or godliness? For it is the God of Abraham, Isaac, and Jacob—the God of all our ancestors—who has brought glory to his servant Jesus by doing this. . . . Through faith in the name of Jesus, this man was healed—and you know how crippled he was before. Faith in Jesus' name has healed him before your very eyes" (Acts 3:12–13, 16 NLT).

What they did, they did by the power of Christ working in and through them, as the branch brings forth fruit by the power of the vine from which comes its life.

But most surely was He seen and known in and by the love His disciples had for one another. "By this all people will know that you are my disciples," said Jesus, "if you have love for one another" (John 13:35 ESV). While they loved they "were of one heart" (Acts 4:32 KJV), and as long as they were of one heart, they were of one mind. Their unity began in the heart, extended to the head, and worked itself out in deeds of loving fellowship and service. Many of them even sold their possessions and had all things in common, so great was their love for the Savior and for each other.

Like the robe of the Master, the infant church was "without seam, woven from the top throughout" (John 19:23 KJV).

The first rip in the seamless robe came when Ananias and his wife, Sapphira, sought credit for a love and generosity of which their wretched hearts were destitute, by pretending to give all when they were holding back part of the price of their sold possession (see Acts 5).

A wider rent was threatened when "the Greek-speaking believers complained about the Hebrew-speaking believers, saying that their widows were being discriminated against in the daily distribution of food" (Acts 6:1 NLT). But this was wisely and promptly arrested by the action of the apostles in appointing "seven men who [were] well respected and [were] full of the Spirit and wisdom" (Acts 6:3 NLT) to look after that business.

The rending of this seamless robe can always be traced back to lack of love. The great heresy of the ages is not manifested so much in false doctrine as in failing love and consequent false living. Faith is lost when love leaks out and living becomes selfish. Heresy begins in the heart, not in the head. The heretic of the early Christian society was the loveless schismatic. "I hear that there are divisions among you," wrote Paul to the Corinthians, "and to some extent I believe it. But, of course, there must be divisions among you so that you who have God's approval will be recognized!" (1 Cor. 11:18–19 NLT).

In the tenth chapter of 1 Corinthians, Paul gave us examples of what befell God's ancient people in the wilderness, and he said, "These things happened to them as examples for us. They were written down to warn us who live at the end of the age" (1 Cor. 10:11 NLT). As we study the history of Israel we see, as types, the things we must do and avoid doing if we would save ourselves and guard the heritage God has given us. Again and again we see the rending or attempted rending of the seamless robe of the ancient people of God. Sometimes it was through envy and jealousy that the rending was attempted. On one occasion Miriam and Aaron would have rent the seamless robe. They spoke against their brother, Moses: "Has the LORD spoken only through Moses? Hasn't he spoken through us, too?" (Num. 12:2 NLT). But the Lord was listening. "The LORD heard them. . . . The LORD was very angry with them" (Num. 12:2, 9 NLT). And Miriam's skin became "as white as snow from leprosy" (Num. 12:10 NLT). Korah and Dathan would also have rent the robe, but again, with sure and swift judgment, God acted as umpire, and Korah and Dathan perished in their presumption (see Num. 16).

Again the rending was attempted by Absalom through unholy ambition. By flattering words and fair promises he sought to steal the hearts of the men of Israel, only to perish in his deceit and pride and have his name handed down through the ages and spit upon as a synonym of unfaithfulness and basest treachery (see 2 Sam. 15).

A fatal rending was finally occasioned by the supercilious pride of those in authority, against which God Himself took up arms. When Solomon's son Rehoboam, turning from the advice of his father's wise old counselors, listened to his young nobles' haughty counsel and declared that his little finger should be thicker than his father's loin, ten tribes forsook him, and ancient Israel was fatally and finally torn asunder and is not yet mended, for to this day the ten tribes are known as the "lost tribes." What the oily duplicity of Absalom failed to accomplish the insolent arrogance of Rehoboam brought to pass. A further rending was caused by the shameless, sinful neglect of those who should have shepherded the sheep. Jeremiah and the lesser prophets wept and lamented and bitterly protested against those who fleece and scatter the sheep instead of feeding and shepherding them, causing the people of God to wander and perish for lack of humble oversight and loving care.

Paul found partiality, favoritism, and a partisan spirit endangering the unity of the seamless robe in Corinth, while at Ephesus he foresaw danger arising from the perversity of those who selfishly sought leadership, and he forewarned them in his farewell address of this danger: "Guard yourselves and God's people. Feed and shepherd God's flock—his church, purchased with his own blood—over which the Holy Spirit has appointed you as elders. I know"—oh, the pity of it!—"that false teachers, like vicious wolves, will come in among you after I leave, not sparing the flock. Even some men from your own group will rise up and distort the truth in order to draw a following" (Acts 20:28–30 NLT), rending the seamless robe to gratify their own lust for leadership.

I think of The Salvation Army as a seamless robe of the Master, beneath whose unrent folds in all lands cluster unnumbered multitudes. Little children, unspoiled as yet, but compassed about with innumerable perils, are there, looking to The Salvation Army for the bread of eternal life whereby their souls shall live, for guidance amid hidden and treacherous snares, and for protection from lurking and watchful foes. Adolescent boys and girls are there, with all their inexplicable moods and trying tempers, their daydreams, their pride and foolishness, their loyalty and rebellions, their ardor and despair, their hopes, their loves, their fun and laziness, their humility, their conceit, their strange insight and hasty judgments, and their sensitiveness and abysmal ignorance—there they are beneath the folds of this seamless robe of the Savior.

Straying girls and wronged women are there. Great sinners, terrible criminals, hopeless outcasts, washed in the blood of the Lamb, are there. Widows and orphans, husbands and wives, bearing burdens of toil and care and anxiety, are there. Aged people, with white hair and feeble steps and dim eyes, are there. The lost and wandering are coming under its worldwide sheltering folds, and for the sake of all these who look trustingly to it for safety and shelter, it must not be torn apart.

For many years, sinister eyes have watched to see it torn in two. Futile attempts have been made by some to rend it, and they have torn off a bit here and there. But the robe still spreads its ample and ever-expanding folds over the nations.

It must not be torn apart, and yet it may be unless we serve the Lord "with all humility of mind" (Acts 20:19 KJV) and in honor prefer others before ourselves, remembering Paul's exhortation to his Philippian brethren: "Complete my joy by being of the same mind, having the same love, being in full accord and of one mind. Do nothing from selfish ambition or conceit, but in humility count others more significant than yourselves" (Phil. 2:2–3 ESV). Let us keep in mind the prayer of Jesus just before the shame and suffering of Pilate's judgment hall and the tragedy of the cross: "I pray that they will all be one, just as you and I are one—as you are in me, Father, and I am in you. And may they be in us so that the world will believe you sent me. . . . I am in them and you are in me. May they experience such perfect unity that the world will know that you sent me and that you love them as much as you love me" (John 17:21, 23 NLT).

May it always be so.

# *Recent Acts of the Holy Spirit* 6

Someone has said that the Acts of the apostles should have been called the Acts of the Holy Spirit because it is there that the personality, work, and leadership of Him who is the "other Comforter" Jesus promised, are made manifest and shown large. And to show that He still works and leads, and makes men and women as triumphant and glad as in those faraway days of the apostles as in the days of Wesley and the early days of The Salvation Army, I want to pass on portions of two letters I recently received, one from an officer and one from a young soldier, one from the Pacific Coast and the other from the Atlantic seaboard.

The first wrote:

I feel I must write and tell you, knowing you will be interested, that on May 3rd of this year God wonderfully sanctified me.

Though for many years I had claimed the blessing, through the preaching of a wonderful man of God, I was shown that there were still carnal propensities dwelling in my heart. I have felt for some time that there was something wrong with my experience. I was not making the progress along spiritual lines I wanted to make, nor was I seeing the success I wanted to see.

That night I saw it all, and though it took me nearly a week to pray through, on the 3rd of May the work was really accomplished in my heart.

What a wonderful peace filled my soul! I never experienced anything like it before. I really received the Holy Ghost that afternoon. He still abides.

As I see my experience now it is like this: About fourteen years ago I claimed the experience and have gone on ever since thinking I had the blessing, but the Devil simply duped me. Though God came to my help when I taught the experience, I was just duped, for I had never really died to sin and really never knew "the old man" to be crucified until the above date.

But now, thank God, there is something more than thinking. The work is done!

When we face our unsatisfactory experience courageously, willing to know the worst about ourselves, and set ourselves to pray before the Lord and to "pray through," the Holy Spirit will surely come and, having come, will abide. But before He can come in to abide, the old sinful nature must be crucified and put off. In closing his letter this brother wrote:

I presume you will remember me as a lieutenant at A_____ when you visited that place thirteen years ago. I remember this incident that occurred at that time. You gave me some letters to put in the post office and stood at the door while I mailed them. I remember distinctly looking at them to see to whom they were addressed. While it was not a sin against God, it was a sin against you and a very great breach of good manners. I want to apologize and ask your pardon.

I do not admit that the brother sinned against me but rather against his own conscience, but this is a fine illustration of the delicacy and tenderness of conscience the Holy Spirit begets, and how courteous and considerate of each other He would make us! And it is because of failure to obey the Spirit in such minor matters that many people are so spiritually coarse and unlovely, or so lean and barren in soul. "The little foxes . . . spoil the vines: for our vines have tender grapes" (Song 2:15 KJV).

The other letter read as follows:

I have been praying for you. As for me, I have entered into a new experience with Jesus. He has lifted me on to a higher plane and showed me things that I never saw before—more light, more love, more peace, more joy, and a better victory.

I have discovered many things about the Devil. It was God's will that I should go through such dark experiences as I wrote you about before. The Lord did not leave me, but He showed me the reality of the Devil and his tricks [see Eph. 6:11]. That certainly was "the slough of lespond," but I came out more than conqueror. Hallelujah!

The Devil surprises me by his perseverance. He is never discouraged. If he can't get the big things, he will try for the small ones. He is putting up a hard fight, but what can he do? The more I fight, the stronger I become and the more I love Jesus. I can't describe to you my experience with Jesus. It is glorious. Hallelujah! He pays me special visits, sometimes in shouting and jumping and the overflowing of the Spirit; and sometimes in calmness with a shower of tears. But, oh, how sweet those tears are! He does not leave me alone, although sometimes I think He does, but I find Him hiding behind that trouble, which He turns into a blessing later.

My heart is flooded with light, love, peace, and joy, and sometimes it is so overflowing that I can't bear it and do not know what to do with myself. Oh, what a change! It began about the time of our correspondence, when you were in C_____, and it is still going higher. The best is yet to come. Hallelujah!

I do not know that I ever saw anyone who had greater darkness and difficulties than this second writer. When I first met him about a year and a half ago, he was full of doubts and questionings and trouble and seemed almost hopelessly in the dark. Again and again he seemed about ready to give up entirely, but with help and encouragement he kept on praying, reading, seeking, and now he has found— and his joy is almost too big for utterance. If people who are not satisfied in their experience would take time to "pray through," they would find their dark tunnels leading out into a large place and into broad day. Jesus still lives and keeps "watch above His own"[1] who hunger to be right. And He pours out the Holy Spirit upon everyone who obeys Him and seeks Him wholeheartedly. But before we can be filled, we must be emptied. Before we can have the "more abundant life," we must die to sin. The old sinful nature must be crucified and put off before Jesus can abide in our hearts and satisfy the hunger of our souls.

Are you satisfied? If not, begin right now and stir up yourself to seek until you have found. Rouse yourself. Find a secret place and pray, and pray again, and yet again, and you shall "pray through" and be satisfied. I know, for I have prayed through. I know, for Jesus has said, "Keep on asking, and you will receive what you ask for. Keep on seeking, and you will find. Keep on knocking, and the door will be opened to you" (Matt. 7:7 NLT). And what Jesus has said is true. What the Lord did for those two writers, He waits and longs to do for you. He is no respecter of persons, and "now is the accepted time" (2 Cor. 6:2 KJV). Say to Him, as Charles Wesley did:

> In vain Thou strugglest to get free,
> I never will unloose my hold!
> Art Thou the Man who died for me?
> The secret of Thy love unfold;
> Wrestling, I will not let Thee go,
> Till I Thy name, Thy nature know.

Yield to me now, for I am weak,

But confident in self-despair;

Speak to my heart, in blessings speak,

Be conquered by my instant prayer;

Speak, or Thou never hence shalt move,

And tell me if Thy name is Love.[2]

And you will soon be crying out as did Wesley:

'Tis Love! 'Tis Love! Thou diedst for me!

I hear Thy whisper in my heart;

The morning breaks, the shadows flee,

Pure, universal love Thou art;

To me, to all, Thy bowels move;

Thy nature and Thy name is Love.[3]

### NOTES

1. James Russell Lowell, "The Present Crisis," 1844, public domain.

2. Charles Wesley, "Come, O Thou Traveler Unknown," 1742, public domain.

3. Ibid.

# The Traveling Evangelist 7

For many years now, my own work has been the work of a traveling evangelist or campaigner. For five years, long before I met The Salvation Army, I resisted the Lord's call to preach. I wanted to be a lawyer and enter politics. To my youthful mind—foolish, darkened, proud, ambitious—all the supreme prizes of life lay in that direction. I respected preachers, but not their job; it looked small to me, not a man's size. But at last a woe—a solemn, inescapable, eternal woe—faced me if I did not preach, and I surrendered.

Then I discovered that there were prizes, positions, and places of power in the ministry. But the job of the evangelist seemed to me to be beneath the dignity of a full-orbed man. Then one day, when in an agony of desire for purity of heart and the baptism of the Holy Spirit, God graciously sanctified me. The Holy Spirit took possession of my yielded, open heart. Christ was revealed in me, and a great passion for the saving and the sanctifying of others burned within me. About that time, a multimillionaire had built one of the finest churches in my native state, and the congregation through him was looking for a pastor. To my surprise I found that the vice president of my old university had recommended me, and one day I received a call to the pastorate of that church. I was elated. I felt that God Himself had opened a great door of opportunity and usefulness to me.

While still considering this call, I went three hundred miles to a holiness convention to sit under the ministry of some great teachers whose books had blessed me. Then God laid His hand upon me, and I knew that I was not to accept the call to that church! I found that which I had least esteemed, had most despised, was the work to which God called me and for which He had set me apart. I must be an evangelist. I felt ordained to this.

I was young, unknown, and in debt for a part of my education. I had no one to advise me. I was utterly alone and had no assurance that any church would welcome my evangelistic services. But on my knees I talked it over with the Lord as I would with an earthly friend and, by faith, into evangelistic work I plunged. Doors opened, and I saw many souls saved and sanctified. From that work, within ten months, I was led into The Salvation Army, where I found myself in London, blacking boots, scrubbing floors, and selling *War Crys*[1] as a cadet in the International Training School. After receiving my commission, I returned to the USA and commanded (in succession) three corps (churches), two divisions (local regions), and was second-in-command of each of the two principal territories in that country, with headquarters in Chicago and New York.

But "the gifts and calling of God are irrevocable" (Rom. 11:29 ESV), and the inner urge to do an evangelist's work was always with me. A great crisis struck The Salvation Army in America.[2] Our ranks were broken. Our people were full of distress and anxious questionings. Our battle line from the Atlantic to the Pacific, three thousand miles long, was in confusion. I felt, when in my office, a consuming desire to get out on the field; to meet our people face-to-face; to hearten, reassure, cheer, exhort, teach, and lead them, the distraught and sore perplexed, into "the fulness of the blessing of the gospel of Christ" (Rom. 15:29 KJV), and to win souls to the Savior. One day I sought and obtained an audience with the Consul,[3] asked her if I might speak to her about myself and my work, and then told her my convictions. Within three months I was appointed as a National Spiritual Special, and for about thirty years now I have been a traveling evangelist.

It has not been an easy job. It has often been lonely and wearying to the point of exhaustion. It has taxed my mind, challenged my will and utmost devotion, drunk up my spirit, and drained me to the dregs till there seemed to be no virtue left in me. And I have had to slip away into solitude, like my Master, to the mountains, for quiet communion and for the replenishing of exhausted reserves of power and the renewing of all life's forces. It has been a fight but not a defeat. I have not been forsaken. His presence has not failed me. He has assured me that the battle was not mine but His, and He has called on me to trust Him and be not afraid. Again and again I have heard His whisper in my heart, "Have I not commanded you? Be strong and courageous. Do not be frightened, and do not be dismayed, for the LORD your God is with you wherever you go" (Josh. 1:9 ESV), and

"Be steadfast, immovable . . . knowing that in the Lord your labor is not in vain" (1 Cor. 15:58 ESV). Sometimes the whisper has been sweet and full of comfort as the tender, cooing voice of a mother to a weary, distressed child. Sometimes it has been sharp and imperative as the staccato notes of a military command on a field of battle. I have not been mollycoddled. I have never for an instant been permitted to think I was God's pet and that I could expect special favors from Him. He has called me to share His cross and to endure hardness as a good soldier, not pleasing myself, not entangling myself with worldly interests or affairs that did not concern me, but to attend strictly to the work He has given me to do.

And now, out of some thirty years of experience as a traveling evangelist, let me write.

A Salvation Army officer told me the story of a wealthy Parsee from India, a silk exporter with great warehouses in Yokohama. After a flood of flame swept over the doomed city, burning to ashes in five hours sixty-nine thousand houses that in five minutes had been cast to the ground by the heaving earth, the officer and others sought the exporter where he had last been seen. All they could find of him was a small streak of ashes. He had been consumed by the fire.

One month before the fire—and the earthquake it accompanied— the Salvation Army officer who told me the story had visited him in his office asking for a donation to help The Salvation Army in its work for sailors in that city. He listened to the officer's plea, and then replied, "If you can tell me one thing you officers of The Salvation Army do which has not as its ultimate object the winning of people to Christ, then I will give you a liberal donation. But you cannot do it;

you wear uniforms, you march the streets, you carry banners, you beat drums and blow instruments, you conduct meetings, you open shelters and soup kitchens, you build citadels, you conduct training colleges, you run rescue homes, you publish books and papers and solicit money for just one object: to help you win souls to Christ and make them followers of Him. I do not believe in Christ. I do not need your Christ. I am rich, but I will give you nothing." A month later the earthquake, the all-consuming fire, and the poor little handful of ashes!

The proud, self-complacent Parsee had grasped the central purpose of The Salvation Army. All its officers and workers have (or should have) this supreme object always in full view. But while there is one spirit and one object, there are manifold ministries to express that spirit and secure that object. There are "the apostles, the prophets, the evangelists, the pastors and teachers" (Eph. 4:11 NIV). Some serve tables as did Stephen, Philip, and others, and some give themselves wholly to the ministry of the word and prayer, as did Peter and the other apostles (see Acts 6:1–8). But all have one object to attain—the winning of souls from sin through faith in Christ, and the binding of them in vital union to Christ and making them channels of His saving grace to others.

The evangelist or "campaigner" is the person who, probably more directly than any other, labors to accomplish this great work. Corps officers, divisional commanders, departmental officers, and territorial leaders have many executive and administrative duties which do not bear so directly upon the saving of souls as does the work of the traveling evangelist. Their work is vitally essential in preparing the way for and conserving the work of soul-winning, but much that they

do bears only indirectly upon the salvation of souls. Campaigners'
work, however, is direct, immediate, unchanging. This one thing they
do (see Phil. 3:13). The burden of caring for the flock, of collecting
and administering finance, erecting buildings, and directing affairs,
do not fall upon them as upon others. Their sole burden, their one
responsibility, is for the souls of men and women. It is a secret burden, a responsibility which is laid upon them and which they assume
in the silence and secret places of their own souls. It is elusive, known
and measured only by God and them. It cannot be measured by a yard-
stick. It cannot be weighed on human scales. It cannot be tabulated in
statistics. Campaigners belong to a divine order, just as prophets and
apostles. They have a divine calling. Their gift is a divine bestow-
ment, and they are among God's gifts to humanity. "These are the
gifts Christ gave to the church: the . . . evangelists" (Eph. 4:11 NLT),
whose sole business is the saving of souls, the perfecting of the saints,
and the building up of the body of Christ on earth, which is composed
of all true Christians.

If we judge the importance of this work in the mind of God by the
place Paul assigns them when he mentions the various orders of
ministry, then they stand next to the apostles and prophets and before
the pastor and teacher.

When we consider this work we will see that this relationship is
perfectly logical. The evangelists receive the revelation, the good
news of God's love and plan of salvation through faith in Christ, from
apostles and prophets, and then by bold and loving presentation of
this revelation, this good news, they win souls and turn them over to
the pastor to be shepherded, and to the teacher to be instructed in the

things of God. Their great work is not the training of souls but the saving of them and, having accomplished this work, they pass on to other fields of labor. They do not erect the building, they provide the material (or, to change the figure, they lay the foundations others build on). They are "fishers of men" (Matt. 4:19 KJV); their business is to catch people. They are reapers of souls on the world's vast harvest fields. That is their one work, and to that they should give themselves with great joy and full and unwearied devotion. They may have other gifts, and if so should not neglect them but cultivate them to the full extent and make them contribute to and support their God-given gift and calling as an evangelist. They should not minimize their calling. They should not vex and discourage themselves by comparing it with that of others, with that of superiors who handle great affairs—as I knew one man to do, much to his own distress and the crippling, in some measure, of his splendid powers.

1. Traveling evangelists should magnify their office. It is true that they are individuals without authority to command and direct others and administer great business, and at times they may be oppressed with a feeling of their own insignificance. But they have spiritual authority, the authority which eternal truth bestows and with which God clothes chosen workers who work and labor in the power of the Holy Spirit. However small they may feel within themselves, they must not minimize their office. Their work is vital. It is God-ordained, and they are walking in the footsteps of the Master who, without any semblance of worldly power or human authority, was the first of their tribe.

Their one weapon is "the sword of the Spirit, which is the word of God" (Eph. 6:17 KJV). Their endowment of power for this work is none less than God the Holy Spirit. The almighty Holy Spirit goes with them to hearten, guide, and give insight, wisdom, courage, boldness in attack, patience in difficulty, and faith and hope in the blackest night. However lonely at times they may feel, they are not alone, "never, no, never alone."[4] They must stir up their faith, recognize the divine Presence, humbly acknowledge their dependence, boldly claim divine help, and draw freely upon the divine resources placed at the disposal of their faith.

It is the special campaigner themselves, and not the details of their campaigns, about which I write. Probably no two people—if left to themselves—would plan an evangelistic campaign exactly alike. Personally, I have never attempted anything spectacular, although I would not discourage this in others. Pageants, spectacular marches and uniforms, striking subjects, special music, all may be most useful to reach the crowd. I have found prayer meetings before a campaign—with personal visitations, announcements, and invitations—most helpful. They stir up interest and a devout, prayerful, expectant spirit that make victory assured.

Campaigners cannot make this initial preparation themselves. Regional and local leaders should do this work in advance of the campaign, and if they do it with heart and soul, and their own hearts are prepared for the visitation of the Spirit, victory is already in sight.

In all my campaigns, it is this preliminary work and this heart preparation for which I have pleaded, and for which I have in secret prayed.

2. Traveling evangelists must spend time and give all diligence to the preparation of their own hearts. If one's own heart is broken, he

or she can then break the hearts of others. If one's own heart is aflame, he or she can kindle a flame in other hearts. A striking program, a brilliant address, or a beautiful song may dazzle the crowd and play on the surface of their emotions, but it is only the passion of the cross that will bring them in contrition and brokenness of heart to the cross. Other things are important, but this preparation of the heart is the one thing without which all other things are empty and vain.

The founder of The Salvation Army, William Booth, always blamed himself if he did not succeed. It is true that other factors are at work for or against the campaign, and the campaigner should not be too quick to assume all the blame of failure. We know there were places where the Master could do no mighty works, because unbelief frustrated Him. And so it may be with us. But usually, if we are warm and tender, joyous and bold, and "full of faith and of the Holy Spirit" (Acts 6:5 ESV), no one will be able to stand before us (see Josh. 1:5). Results rich and enduring will reward our labor.

We must study to show ourselves approved unto God, workers who need not be ashamed (see 2 Tim. 2:15). God is not a hard Master, but He will not—cannot—lightly approve us. We must not presume on His goodwill, but with all watchfulness and diligence so work that He can approve, and that our hearts will not condemn, but will reassure us.

3. Traveling evangelists must exercise their spiritual senses lest, having eyes to see, they see not, and having ears to hear, they hear not (see Ezek. 12:2). They must have eyes that pierce through appearances, that can see the horses and chariots of fire where others see only the arrogant, encircling hosts of Syria. They must have ears to

hear the assuring voice of their Captain and distinguish it from the voices of self-interest, of expediency, and of the fiend who sometimes simulates and is "transformed into an angel of light" (2 Cor. 11:14 KJV).

The author of Hebrews spoke approvingly of those "who by reason of use have their senses exercised to discern both good and evil" (Heb. 5:14 KJV). But beyond discernment of good and evil, the campaigner must have eyes to see victory where others see foredoomed defeat. The smallest crowd may have immeasurable possibilities in it. A Luther, Wesley, or William Booth may be looking out through the eyes of some little child or some awkward, shy, or mischievous, adolescent boy. An Elizabeth Fry, Catherine Booth, or Hannah Ouchterlony may spring forth from the chrysalis of some reserved girl who listens with rapt attention. Personally, I seldom speak to a congregation without thinking that I may be directly or indirectly addressing someone who shall yet be a prophet of the Highest, a herald to nations. Possibly I have been somewhat influenced by the results of my first sermon in my first appointment as a young preacher. In that first service, two people—a young man and a young woman—yielded to Christ, and the young man, principal of the public school, preached for me before the end of the year and went later as a missionary to India. Sometimes we reach them indirectly. We get some "nobody" saved and God uses that nobody to reach somebody who becomes great in the Lord's sight. Let us have no hesitancy in permitting our spiritual imagination to reinforce our faith and enkindle our hope and so sustain our courage in the face of massed and mocking foes and threatened defeat.

4. Traveling evangelists must be humble. They must seek nothing for themselves but be willing for others to carry off the so-called

prizes of this life. They are not "lords over God's heritage"; they are shepherds of the sheep, "examples to the flock" (1 Pet. 5:3 KJV). They hold no dominion over the faith of others, but are helpers of their joy (see 2 Cor. 1:24). Like John the Baptist, they are quite willing to decrease, if only Christ increases. Their joy is that of the friend of the Bridegroom (see John 3:29–30). Like Paul they are jealous for others "with the deep concern of God himself," desiring above all things that their "love should be for Christ alone, just as a pure maiden saves her love for one man only, for the one who will be her husband," but also frightened that they will be led away from a "pure and simple devotion to our Lord, just as Eve was deceived by Satan" (2 Cor. 11:2–3 TLB). And like Epaphras, they labor fervently in prayer that their spiritual progeny may stand perfect and complete in all the will of God (see Col. 4:12).

5. Finally, traveling evangelists—coming to an area or church with no power to command but only to preach and pray, to help and inspire, and to seek the lost—should be received as God's messengers, supported by love and prayers and understanding sympathy, and helped in their mission in every possible way, that Christ may be glorified, souls won, little children gathered into the fold, and all brothers and sisters quickened and sanctified.

## NOTES

1. The flagship publication of The Salvation Army, published in many different versions around the world.

2. In 1896 Ballington Booth, son of the founders, William and Catherine Booth, resigned as national commander of The Salvation Army in the United States and, taking some personnel and property along with him, started the Volunteers of America.

3. Emma Booth-Tucker, who with her husband Frederick Booth-Tucker, was appointed to succeed Ballington and Maud Booth as national commanders of The Salvation Army in the US.

4. Ludie Carrington Day Pickett, "Never Alone," 1897, public domain.

# *Must You Be Fed with a Spoon?* 8

I am watching with much interest and some personal profit the development of my grandchildren. They are a luxury to my old heart but, like all children, they are somewhat of a problem as well as a joy to their parents. At first, when brought to the table, they were fed with a spoon, but one day the spoon was put into their tiny hands and they were permitted to feed themselves. I was fascinated. The spoon would plunge into the porridge or applesauce and come up at various and sundry angles and start on a wobbling journey to the sweet, wee, wide-open mouth. Sometimes it would hit and sometimes it would miss. If it reached the open mouth, well. Its contents were soon lost in the dark "little red lane" below. But if it missed, or if there were miscalculation as to time and the mouth closed before the spoon arrived, it was awesome. The little mouth closed on air, and another plunge and wobbling effort was made. The bib and plate and platter were often a fearsome sight, and the small face was often battered and buttered in a way that was a joy to behold, but they were learning. It was the only way they could learn. They could not always be fed with a spoon by others. They must feed themselves, and someday they may have to feed others. But their first lesson is to feed themselves. Of course, their food is all prepared for them by other hands. But the day will come when they will not only have to feed themselves, but they may have to prepare their own food. But before the food can be prepared, it must be found. The farmer must cultivate the soil and raise wheat and corn. The fisherman must catch the fish. The horticulturist must grow the fruit. The herdsmen must raise the cattle and sheep. And it is just possible that in some far-off day these children must not only feed themselves and prepare the food, but also go out and find the food to prepare and eat. Or they may toil for the money with which to buy from those who have labored to produce.

The feeding of men and women is a complex process, which we may live a lifetime without considering, but which is most instructive and humbling to consider.

Can you feed your own soul or must you still be fed? Do you prepare your own soul food or do others prepare it for you? Do you labor for it or do others give it to you?

One Salvation Army divisional commander said, "I will guarantee I can send the worst kind of backslidden officers to a certain corps, and in three months the soldiers will have prayed for them and helped them and loved them and gotten them so blessed that they will be on fire for God and souls."

Those soldiers were no longer spiritual babies who had to be fed with a spoon. No doubt they had vigorous spiritual appetites and enjoyed a meal of "strong meat" (Heb. 5:12 KJV) prepared for them. But they were no longer dependent. They were independent. They were no longer babes in Christ. They had exercised their senses (see Heb. 5:14) and become spiritual men and women, able to feed themselves, able to prepare their own food, and able to work and forage for themselves and find their own food. And not only so, but they were able to feed others. If their officers did not give them suitable soul food, then they fed the officers. If nobody blessed them, then they rose up in their splendid spiritual man- and womanhood and blessed somebody else, and so blessed themselves. Like the widow of Zarephath, who divided her poor little handful of meal and her few spoonsful of oil with Elijah and found the meal and oil unwasting through months of famine (see 1 Kings 17), so they gave of their spiritual food to more needy souls and found themselves enriched from God's unfailing supplies.

I know one of the finest Salvation Army bands in the USA, composed of a splendid group of soldiers, who for years would not have— and for all I know, to this day will not have—as a band member one who did not have the blessing of a clean heart. They said, "We want our band to be not only a combination of musical instruments, but also of harmonious hearts. We want to produce melody from our hearts as from our instruments. We cannot have discord in our band. We must have sweetest harmony." And so, before anyone was admitted as a member of the band, that person must not only give evidence of the ability to play an instrument, but also show the ability to live peaceably, humbly, lovingly, and loyally with others. They were prepared to pray with him or her and lead this person into the blessed experience of holiness, perfect love, purity and power, and then gladly accept him or her as a member of the band. They could feed themselves and others too. And that band became a great spiritual influence in that city and famous for a hundred miles around.

One day Paul came to Corinth and found a man named Aquila and his wife, Priscilla, and he lived and worked with them, because they were tentmakers just as he was. But they later moved to Ephesus, and then one day an eloquent man named Apollos, who was mighty in the Scriptures, fervent in spirit, and speaking and teaching diligently the things of the Lord, came to the city. He was a great orator, teacher, and preacher. But this humble tentmaker and his wife had learned more from Paul than Apollos knew, so they invited him home to dinner with them, "and expounded unto him the way of the Lord more perfectly" (Acts 18:26 KJV).

Aquila and Priscilla had learned to feed themselves and others too—even such a man as Apollos, eloquent, burning with zeal and mighty in the Scriptures. They must have had fullness of love and very gracious ways, and a divine tact to approach a great man like that and lead him into fullness of blessing. Oh, that we were all like that!

One evening I found myself sitting with a fellow Salvation Army officer after a soul-stirring meeting on our way to our lodgings.

"I was at the penitent form [the kneeler for confession]," he said.

"Were you? I missed you and wondered where you were." I had seen him sitting down in the audience while the speaker poured out his heart in a torrent of searching truth upon the crowd. There was a look on his face that puzzled me. I was not sure whether defiance, cynicism, questioning, indifference, or soul hunger was revealed in that look. When the prayer meeting began, every head was bowed, but he sat erect with that puzzling look in his face intensified. People were melting and flowing down to the penitent form, but still he sat erect, open-eyed, apparently unmoved. I knelt to deal with seekers, and when I looked again he was gone, and not until after the meeting did I learn that he had been to the penitent form.

"Yes, I was at the penitent form. An old officer came and asked if he could help me, but I told him, 'No, I want to be left alone.' I was vexed; half angry."

"Angry! What were you angry about?"

"Well, while I listened to the speaker, I wondered, 'Why don't our leaders feed us young fellows? They don't have meetings with us. Why don't they help us?'"

I had up to that time thought of him as a youngster. He belongs to the younger set of officers. I had known him since he was a small lad, and I had always thought of him as a young man, but when he called himself a "young fellow" my mind turned a somersault. I looked at him and asked, "How old are you?"

"Thirty-five."

"And you have been married thirteen years and have a family of children, the oldest of whom is twelve. You are not a young fellow. You are a middle-aged man. And you want your leaders to feed you. But that is not what you need. You need to feed yourself. Your leaders cannot tell you anything you do not know. But do you diligently practice what you know? You don't pray enough. You do not search the Scriptures and feed on the Word of God as you should. 'Man shall not live by bread alone, but by every word . . . of God' [Matt. 4:4 NKJV]. Is not that your trouble? Do you deny yourself as you should? Do you search for soul food in good books? Or do you not spend more time reading the sporting page of the morning and evening papers than you spend over your Bible and books that would enrich your mind and heart? Are you not starving yourself and waiting for someone to come and feed you, when you should be feeding yourself?"

I once knew a man who, when I first met him, was sodden with drink. But within a few days he was saved and sanctified. Shortly after, he became an officer, and then got himself a small but choice library of the most deeply spiritual books. He would sit up till after midnight reading, praying, and meditating on what he read, until in a short time I marveled at him. His mind was all alert, his soul was on fire, and his mental and spiritual equipment was a joy to those who knew him. He labored for spiritual food, and grew in mental and spiritual stature and in favor with God and man. And he was soon able to feed others. Whenever I met him, he wanted to talk about spiritual things. His grasp of doctrine, his knowledge of Scripture and holiness literature, and his intimate acquaintance and communion with God delighted and refreshed me. He was an ordinary country boy, but he became extraordinary by the diligence with which he sought fellowship with God, the eagerness with which he hunted for truth from books and from experienced people, and the loving zeal with which he sought to impart the truth to other souls about him.

Wise old Nehemiah said, "Go your way, eat the fat, and drink the sweet, and send portions unto them for whom nothing is prepared" (Neh. 8:10 KJV).

Learn to feed yourself, and also to share your soul food with yet needier souls, and so you shall know no soul famine, but be "fat and flourishing" (Ps. 92:14 KJV).

One of the outstanding ironies of history is the utter disregard of ranks and titles in the final judgments human beings pass upon each other. And if this is so of us, how much more must it be so of the judgments of God.

Nero and Marcus Aurelius each sat upon the throne of Rome clothed with absolute power and worshiped as gods, but what a difference! Nero, a monster of iniquity and utter cruelty, execrated of all; Aurelius, a vigorous administrator and benign philosopher, writing meditations which the wise and learned still delight to read and ponder and which after two millennia are a guide to safe and useful living.

Napoleon and Washington were two great statesmen and military leaders. But what a difference! One a ruthless conqueror, building a glittering and evanescent empire on an ocean of blood, dying an exile on a lonely isle with a character for heartless selfishness which sinks lower and lower every year in the estimation of all right-thinking people. The other refusing a crown, but laying the firm foundations of a state destined to be infinitely greater than Napoleon's empire, and dying at last honored by his former foes, with a character above reproach, revered and beloved of all.

Judas and John were two apostles. But what a difference! One was a devil, betraying his Master with a kiss for a paltry handful of silver and making his name a synonym for all infamy and treachery. The other pillowed his head on the Master's bosom and with wide open eyes was permitted to look deep into heaven, behold the great white throne and Him who sat upon it, the worshiping angel hosts, the innumerable multitudes of the redeemed, the glory of the Lamb that was slain, and the face of the everlasting Father, while his name became a synonym for reverence and adoring love.

This summing up and final estimate of these men shows that history cares not an iota for rank or title, but only for the quality of one's deeds and the character of one's mind and heart.

The haughty patricians of Rome doubtless passed by with contemptuous indifference or scorn as the scarred Jewish prisoner, Paul, with sore eyes and wearied feet, went clanking by in chains to the dungeon. But their names have perished, while his name is enshrined in millions of hearts and embalmed in colleges, cathedrals, and cities, and libraries of books are reverently written about his character, his sufferings, and his work.

Who remembers the Lord Bishops of England in Bunyan's day? But what unnumbered Christian hearts have turned with tears of deepest gratitude and tenderest affection and sympathy to the humble, joyous, inspired tinker, who from the filthy, verminous Bedford jail sent forth his immortal story of Pilgrim fleeing from the city of destruction?

How many recall Pilgrim as he escaped with hopes and fears and tears and prayers and sighs and songs, pressing on over hills of difficulty, through sloughs of despond, past bewitching bowers of beguiling temptations and giants of despair and castles of doubt, till at last he beheld the delectable mountains, viewed not far away the city of the great King, heard the music of celestial harpers playing on their harps of gold, and, passing through the swelling river, was received with glad welcome on the other shore!

Those whom history acclaims, posterity reveres, and God crowns are those who put first things first, to whom first things have first place in all their thoughts, plans, affections, and activities.

So what shall be first with us? Many hands stretch out toward us, and many voices plead with us for first place. Which shall have the primacy? Which shall have our last thoughts when falling asleep at night and our first thoughts on awaking in the morning?

There are many things that make so subtle and apparently so reasonable an appeal that, if we do not watch and pray and keep in the Spirit, they will usurp first place, and we shall someday wake up and find that we have been bowing down to an idol instead of to the living God.

We may put our work first. Is it not commanded, "Whatever your hand finds to do, do it with your might" (Eccl. 9:10 ESV)? And aren't we exhorted to be "not slothful in business" (Rom. 12:11 KJV)? And are we not assured that "a man who excels in his work . . . will stand before kings" (Prov. 22:29 NKJV)? Is not our work God's work? And can anything equal it in importance? Are we not warned that if we are careless we shall be cursed? If we are slothful, our talent shall be taken from us, given to another, and we ourselves cast out into outer darkness as wicked and slothful servants, where we shall fruitlessly weep and gnash our teeth. Is not our work the building of God's kingdom on earth, the rescue of men and women from sin and its eternal woe? Yes, yes, yes, it is all that, and no words can express the infinity of its importance. But it must not have first place. If it does, we ourselves shall be lost. "On judgment day many will say to me, 'Lord! Lord! We prophesied in your name and cast out demons in your name and performed many miracles in your name.' But I will reply, 'I never knew you'" (Matt. 7:22–23 NLT). Solemn words these, spoken by the Master.

Many years ago, I was billeted with one of the most brilliant and capable staff officers I have known. We had had a great meeting that night and got to bed late and wearied but, according to my custom, I was up early the next morning, seeking God, reading my Bible, and praying. The blessing of the Lord came upon me and I burst into tears. My companion woke up and found me praying, weeping, and rejoicing. He was much moved and confessed to me that he did not often sense that he had found God when he was praying, and explained that he was so busy, so pressed with his work, so absorbed and fascinated with it, that when he prayed his mind wandered to things he should do during the day so he seldom got into real touch and fellowship with God. I earnestly warned him of the danger this meant to his own soul and eventually to his work, the dryness and spiritual barrenness that must come upon him if, through the multiplicity of cares and the pressure of work, God was crowded out or pushed into the background of his life. He admitted the truth of all I said, but he still put his work first. He rose rapidly in rank and important command, then suddenly dropped out of his ministry over some trifling matter and has long been dead. Did his exceptionally bright and promising career end in darkness because he failed to put first things first? I have feared so.

It is possible to so far lose sight of first things that we come at last to do much if not all our work with an eye to our own promotion and future career. We may become embittered toward our leaders and jealous toward our coworkers if we are not promoted as rapidly as others, or if our position does not correspond to what we consider our due. It is a most subtle danger, and through it many a person's splendid spiritual career has come to an end, while he or she yet goes on in a perfunctory performance of official duties, beating time, moving but not progressing, doing no vital and lasting work for God and souls. Of such it could be written, "You have the reputation of being alive, but you are dead" (Rev. 3:1 ESV). I have met people who spent more time repining and complaining and inwardly rebelling about not being promoted than they did in studying and working and fitting themselves for the work that promotion would thrust upon them. "It's not good to seek honors for yourself," wrote Solomon (Prov. 25:27 NLT), but such people quite overlook such texts as that, and while they may attain the desire of their heart, they miss the glory that God gives.

Personally, an awful fear has shaken me at times—the thought that a person may get in this world all the honor and glory that he or she seeks, and find in the next world that there is nothing further coming, like workers who draw an advance on their salary and at the end of the week or month or year have nothing to receive. In the story of the rich man and Lazarus, Abraham said to the rich man, "Son, remember that during your lifetime you had everything you wanted" (Luke 16:25 NLT) and there was nothing due to him in that new world to which his soul had been so suddenly snatched away. He had not put first things first, and he who proudly scorned the poor beggar Lazarus at his gate now found himself an eternal pauper and beggar in hell.

We may gradually put our family first. It has been said that until the age of forty-five we say, "What can I do to advance myself?" After forty-five we say, "What can I do to provide for and advance my children?" However, this may become a deadly snare. Parents' ambition or anxiety may override sober judgment and compromise their devotion to God's cause. "Whoever loves son or daughter more than me is not worthy of me," said Jesus (Matt. 10:37 ESV).

We may put our own culture first. This is not a widespread danger among us, and yet it may become to some a very subtle danger. Study, reading, travel, the cultivation of the mind, and the gratifying of taste may lead to the neglect of God's work and the drying up of the fountains of spiritual power. Personal growth is not to be despised, but rather coveted. The better informed and the wiser and more cultivated we are, provided we are dedicated wholly to God and set on fire with spiritual passion, the more effectually can we glorify God and serve others. It is true that "God chose things the world considers foolish in order to shame those who think they are wise. And he chose things that are powerless to shame those who are powerful. God chose things despised by the world, things counted as nothing at all, and used them to bring to nothing what the world considers important. As a result, no one can ever boast in the presence of God" (1 Cor. 1:27–29 NLT). But

He also chose Moses, educated in all the learning of Egypt, the most cultured man of his age, and Paul, educated at the universities of Tarsus and Jerusalem, for the great work of the ages. Not many such has God chosen, because not often do such cultured individuals choose Christ and the cross. But God can and does use culture, when dedicated wholly to His service, and we should not despise it, but covet it and take every legitimate opportunity to secure it. But woe to those who put it first in their thought and effort. God will laugh at such people, pass them by, and give their crowns to little illiterate nobodies who love, trust, shout, sing, know nothing but Jesus Christ and His crucifixion, and count not their lives dear to themselves, wanting only that they may win the souls for whom the Savor died.

If we would put first things first, we must be ready at any moment to lay aside our books, our music, our studies, our business, and our own pleasure and profit to save souls.

The founder of The Salvation Army, William Booth, on the train in Switzerland, was writing an article when members of his staff called him to look at the Alps towering upward into the blue heavens, gleaming in white, majestic splendor. But his heart and mind were so absorbed with his work and the greater splendors of the Spirit, and of redeeming love, that he would hardly lift his eyes from the work in which he was lost. Again and again I have had to practice this kind of stern self-denial in my world travels if I would keep first things first.

Museums which house the symbols of a nation's history and the products of its genius and labor are a medium of culture. I once spent two weeks within two or three stone-throws of one of Europe's national museums, and passing it on several occasions, longed to run in and spend some time among its strange and ancient treasures. But a mighty work of the Spirit was going on, my time was short, and hungry souls so thronged me, both in and between the meetings, that I had to deny them or deny myself the pleasure and instruction I might have found in that treasure house of science and art and natural wonders. To some it might have made no appeal. To me it did, but it was denied in order that first things might have first place, and any regret for my loss is swallowed up in the joy of my greater gain and the gain of those precious souls to whom I ministered.

This demand that first things shall have first place is not simply a demand of the spiritual life, but of all life, of every profession and activity. The soldier must not entangle him- or herself with the secular affairs of life. The lawyer must make law his or her mistress and give it full devotion. The physician must put the profession of healing before all business or pleasure. The student must deny him- or herself and hold everything secondary to studies. The true lover must forsake all others for the one who is enshrined in his or her heart's best affections.

What, then, shall be first in our thoughts, our affections, our life? What must be placed first is that which, were we to lose it, would mean the loss of all. To lose God is the sum of all loss. If we lose Him, we lose all. If we lose all and still have Him, we shall in Him again find all. "I once thought these things were valuable," wrote Paul, "but now I consider them worthless because of what Christ has done. Yes, everything else is worthless when compared with the infinite value of knowing Christ Jesus my Lord. For his sake I have discarded everything else, counting it all as garbage" (Phil. 3:7–8 NLT). And yet this poor man, persecuted, hated, hunted, stripped of all things, cried out to his brothers in like poverty, "All things are yours: whether Paul, or Apollos, or Cephas, or the world, or life, or death, or things present, or things to come—all are yours. And ye are Christ's, and Christ is God's" (1 Cor. 3:21–23 KJV).

"Seek me and live" (Amos 5:4 ESV) is God's everlasting plea to you and me. Uzziah sought God and "as long as he sought the LORD, God made him to prosper. . . . He was marvellously helped, till he was strong. But when he was strong, his heart was lifted up to his destruction: for he transgressed against the LORD his God" (2 Chron. 26:5, 15–16 KJV).

What a grim, revealing glimpse we have in those words, down the long, dim vista of three millennia into the secret of that old king's glory and doom! And "they were written down for our instruction, on whom the end of the ages has come" (1 Cor. 10:11 ESV).

Many years ago I heard the founder of The Salvation Army, in an impassioned plea to his people to wait on God, cry out, "Men are losing God every day, and I should lose Him if out of my busy life I did not take time every day to seek His face." And in a letter quoted by Harold Begbie, he wrote:

> I wish I could have a little more time for *meditation* about *eternal* things. I must not let my soul get dried up with secular affairs—even though they concern the highest earthly interests of my fellows. After all, *soul* matters are of infinite importance and are really most closely concerned with earthly advantages.[1]

If it was so with King Uzziah and with our revered founder, it is so with us! These men, though dead, yet speak to us. And though they came back to us as the rich man who begged Abraham for Lazarus to come back with warning to his brothers, yet they could have no other message, they could not speak otherwise. They have spoken their final word, and to me, at least, it is the word of the Lord.

As the psalmist said, "When You said, 'Seek My face,' my heart said to You, 'Your face, LORD, I will seek'" (Ps. 27:8 NKJV).

Thou, O Christ, art all I want,

More than all in Thee I find.[2]

## NOTES

1. Harold Begbie, *The Life of General William Booth: The Founder of The Salvation Army* (London: Macmillan and Company, 1926), 234.

2. Charles Wesley, "Jesus, Lover of My Soul," 1740, public domain.

# *God Is Faithful* 10

A devout woman wrote me a letter from Texas recently and said, "My text for today is, 'He that is faithful in that which is least is faithful also in much; and he that is unjust [unrighteous] in the least is unjust [unrighteous] also in much' (Luke 16:10 KJV)."

What searching words of the Savior are those! They should give us pause. They should set us to searching and judging ourselves. And this searching should enter into all departments of our lives. This judgment should be as before God's eyes, it should be unsparing—far more so than our judgment upon our neighbors. When we judge them, we may do ourselves and them great harm and injustice and bring upon ourselves judgment and condemnation, for we are bidden not to sit in judgment upon others. "Judge not," said Jesus (Matt. 7:1 KJV). "Who are you to judge your neighbor?" wrote James (James 4:12 ESV). But if we candidly and impartially judge ourselves, we may thereby do ourselves and others great good and so escape the judgment of God, for "if we judged ourselves truly"—and so correct ourselves—"we would not be judged," wrote Paul (1 Cor. 11:31 ESV).

So if we would be "faithful in that which is least," what are some of the least things?

Are we faithful in the use of money? Jesus was talking about business and money when He spoke of being "faithful in that which is least." Personally, I have for many years felt that one-tenth of all I had belonged to God. A distinguished Christian leader said to me one day, "You have given yourself to God, why give Him your money?" I confess I was deeply surprised, if not shocked. I ask others to give, and I would feel myself utterly faithless if I did not give freely to my Master's cause and to His poor as I am able.

Are we faithful in the use of our time? Do we gather up the minutes for some useful employment, for prayer, for reading, for visiting? Some people waste much time at night which they should spend in bed, and then they waste much time in bed the next morning when they should be up studying, praying, rejoicing, and attending to the day's duties.

Are we faithful in our speech? Little words are continually slipping out through the portals of our lips. Are they words we would say in Jesus' presence? I was much struck recently as I read Psalm 12, in which God confronted people over their words and they proudly and insolently replied, "Our lips are our own—who can stop us?" (Ps. 12:4 NLT). "The tongue is a small thing," wrote the apostle James (James 3:5 NLT). Are we faithful in its use, or are we careless, thoughtless, foolish, and wicked? For every idle, harmful word we shall have to give an account and we shall be brought into judgment, said the Master (see Matt. 12:36). Oh, how important it is to be faithful in our speech.

Are we faithful in the use of eyes and ears and hands and feet? Are we faithful with ourselves, our hearts, our consciences, our imaginations? Do we live as in God's sight, seeking always to do the things that please Him, so that we have the sweet, silent whisper in our hearts, "My beloved child in whom I am well pleased"?

The apostle John wrote to "the beloved Gaius. . . . Beloved, you do faithfully whatever you do" (3 John 1, 5 NKJV). If you and I do likewise, someday a greater one than John will say to us, "Well done, good and faithful servant. You have been faithful over a little; I will set you over much. Enter into the joy of your master" (Matt. 25:23 ESV).

# *The Bible and Religious Experience*  11

We do not discover God. God reveals Himself to us. God seeks us before we seek God. God reveals His wisdom and power through nature. He reveals His holiness through conscience. He reveals His hatred of sin through His judgments. He reveals His redeeming love through faith. We see God's power in starry heavens, storm-swept seas, rushing rivers, lofty mountains, flaming volcanoes, devastating tornadoes, and in the silent forces irresistibly lifting mighty forests from tiny seeds and holding them aloft in columnar strength and beauty against wind and storm from century to century.

We see the wisdom of God in the marvelous adaptations of nature: the way the eye responds to light and color, the ear to sound, the nose to odors, the tongue to flavors, the skin to heat and cold; how the thumb and fingers set ever so aptly against each other; the processes of the organs of digestion and peristaltic and cardiac action; the varieties of plants and animals; the differences between individuals; and the bond of mother and child.

We see the redeeming love of God in Christ, in His works of pity and mercy, but most clearly in His atoning death on the cross.

But all this manifold unveiling and revelation of Himself God sums up in His Word. He declares Himself in the Scriptures, and therein we see Him as though reflected in a perfect mirror. We read, "The LORD revealed himself to Samuel in Shiloh by the word of the LORD" (1 Sam. 3:21 KJV). He declares His power, His wisdom, His knowledge, His holiness, His righteousness, His mercy, His everlasting love, His redeeming purpose, and His plan in His Word. And this Word is vitally related to all satisfying and assured Christian experience. It floods the Christian with light. It reveals to us God's benevolent and passionately active interest in us. It shows the way and spirit in which to seek God, and the condition of pardon, purity, and power. And when we have met these conditions, the Holy Spirit applies the words of Scripture to our hearts with life-giving energy, so that that text in Proverbs is fulfilled in our experience: "When you walk, their counsel will lead you. When you sleep, they will protect you. When you wake up, they will advise you" (Prov. 6:22 NLT).

Nature only partially reveals God, and the wisest people stumble and falter in trying to interpret God through nature. But in the Word of God we find Him fully and plainly revealed to the obedient and trusting soul.

But even the Scriptures fail to reveal God in all His beauty unless with penitence and faith we have drawn near to Him, been born from above, and been sanctified by the incoming of the Holy Spirit. The Book is in large measure sealed to unspiritual minds.

When Jesus prayed, "Father, bring glory to your name," we read that a voice came from heaven, saying, "I have already brought glory to my name, and I will do so again" (John 12:28 NLT), and people interpreted the voice according to their spiritual condition and relationship. "Some thought it was thunder"—a material interpretation; it had no spiritual significance to them. Others said "an angel had spoken to him"—a spiritualistic interpretation. Only Jesus heard the voice of the everlasting Father. "The voice was for your benefit, not mine," said He (John 12:29–30 NLT).

> Where one heard noise, and one saw flame,
> I only knew He named my name.[1]

One person will read the Old Testament and see nothing but myths; scraps of legendary history; folklore; a record of dreams; bits of biography; exaggerated stories of fights, battles, and wars of semi-savage tribes; and songs of a people slowly emerging from barbarism into civilization.

Another will read it and discover God down among His wayward creatures in their spiritual childhood revealing Himself to them in dreams, visions, judgments, deliverances, special providence, and His Word through His prophets, as they were able to bear the great unveiling, until at last the final and full revelation came in Christ: "In the past God spoke to our ancestors through the prophets at many times and in various ways, but in these last days he has spoken to us by his Son" (Heb. 1:1–2 NIV).

Well may we pray David's prayer (I have prayed it a thousand times): "Open my eyes that I may see wonderful things in your law"

(Ps. 119:18 NIV). And well may we covet the experience of the disciples: "Then he opened their minds to understand the Scriptures" (Luke 24:45 ESV).

It was this that happened to Paul on the road to Damascus (see Acts 9). His spiritual eyes were opened. He saw God in Christ, and the old Scriptures with which he was so familiar took on new meaning, so that he said, "Whatever was written in former days was written for our instruction, that through endurance and through the encouragement of the Scriptures we might have hope" (Rom. 15:4 ESV). When he read the story of the wanderings of his people in the wilderness on their way from Egypt to the land of promise, and how they were overthrown and perished in the wilderness, he recognized God's displeasure and saw a warning example: "Now these things took place as examples for us, that we might not desire evil as they did. . . . They were written down for our instruction, on whom the end of the ages has come" (1 Cor. 10:6, 11 ESV). And to Timothy he wrote, "All Scripture is inspired by God and is useful to teach us what is true and to make us realize what is wrong in our lives. It corrects us when we are wrong and teaches us to do what is right. God uses it to prepare and equip his people to do every good work" (2 Tim. 3:16–17 NLT).

It was this that happened to Martin Luther as on his knees he painfully climbed the stairway in St. Peter's in Rome, and the still small voice sounded in his soul: "The just shall live by faith" (Rom. 1:17 KJV). Scales dropped from the eyes of his soul, God's kindly purpose and way of salvation by faith was seen, and the Scriptures flamed with new and spiritual meaning and became the passionate study of his remaining years.

It was this that happened to Augustine, the brilliant young rhetorician and libertine of Carthage, as—deeply convicted of sin and spiritual impotence—he walked in his garden. He heard a voice in his inner ear that said, "Take and read." And taking up Paul's letter to the Romans he read, "The night is far gone; the day is at hand. So then let us cast off the works of darkness and put on the armor of light. Let us walk properly as in the daytime, not in orgies and drunkenness, not in sexual immorality and sensuality, not in quarreling and jealousy. But put on the Lord Jesus Christ, and make no provision for the flesh, to gratify its desires" (Rom. 13:12–14 ESV). Instantly his inner being flamed with spiritual light. The chains of his fleshly lusts and evil habits fell off, the dungeon doors of his soul flew open, he walked out into the broad day of God's deliverance and salvation, and the Scriptures henceforth were a lamp to his feet (see Ps. 119:105).

The Word of the Lord came in searching experiences and travailings of spirit as God drew near and revealed His will, His name, and His nature to men and women. It came not "from human initiative," wrote Peter. "No, those prophets were moved by the Holy Spirit, and they spoke from God." And he assures us that "because of that experience, we have even greater confidence in the message proclaimed by the prophets. You must pay close attention to what they wrote, for their words are like a lamp shining in a dark place—until the Day dawns, and Christ the Morning Star shines in your hearts" (2 Pet. 1:19–21 NLT).

Ezekiel said, "The word of the LORD came unto me" (Ezek. 3:16 KJV).

Jeremiah wrote, "The word of the LORD came unto me" (Jer. 1:4 KJV).

The book of Genesis says, "Now the LORD had said unto Abraham" (Gen. 12:1 KJV).

And later Jeremiah wrote, "The LORD appeared to us in the past, saying: 'I have loved you with an everlasting love; I have drawn you with unfailing kindness'" (Jer. 31:3 NIV).

The Bible is inspired. There has been much questioning and debate about the nature and extent of biblical inspiration. Some Bible lovers maintain that every word was given by inspiration, while others have argued that the writers chose their own words in which to express the thoughts and revelations welling up within them. But a thoughtful study seems to plainly show that some of the words were given while others were chosen by the writers.

Paul was troubled with a thorn in the flesh, and three times prayed for deliverance from it. Then Jesus spoke to him, and Paul gave us His very words which, translated, read: "My grace is all you need. My power works best in weakness." Those words so assured and satisfied and inspired Paul that he cried out, "So now I am glad to boast about my weaknesses, so that the power of Christ can work through me. That's why I take pleasure in my weaknesses, and in the insults, hardships, persecutions, and troubles that I suffer for Christ. For when I am weak, then I am strong" (2 Cor. 12:9–10 NLT). There is no reason to suppose that those exact words were put into Paul's mouth. It is sufficient to know that the words of Jesus thrilled and cheered and inspired him into glad submission to the will and purpose of God in his affliction, and in his joy and satisfaction his heart overflowed with devotion to his Lord and found verbal expression in these words.

One day the psalmist was so filled with the sense of God's forgiving love and provident care that his whole soul bubbled over in song, and he cried out: "Bless the LORD, O my soul, and all that is within me, bless his holy name! Bless the LORD, O my soul, and forget not all his benefits, who forgives all your iniquity, who heals all your diseases, who redeems your life from the pit, who crowns you with steadfast love and mercy, who satisfies you with good so that your youth is renewed like the eagle's" (Ps. 103:1–5 ESV).

Those words are the words of the writer, but they are written in the glad sense of all God's tender care and goodness and redeeming love, out of a heart that is inspired by the ever-present Holy Spirit to adoring worship and praise. The words are the words of the writer, but the rich experience and deep feelings and adoring wonder from which they flowed are the work and inspiration of the Holy One of Israel.

"I know the Bible is inspired," wrote a great soul-winner, "because it inspires me."[2] And so it does to everyone who, wholly devoted to Christ and simply trusting, is filled with the Spirit. It speaks as the very voice of God. God is in the Word and "the very words . . . are spirit and life" (John 6:63 NLT).

The manner and extent of inspiration may always be a matter of debate, but the fact of inspiration is the joy and strength of every "twice-born" soul.

The Bible is invaluable in personal dealing. "You will always have the poor among you," said the Master (John 12:8 NLT), and we must wisely and adequately minister to their pitiful and crying words. But it is equally probable that the feeble-minded and the weak will be ever with us. And Paul has exhorted and instructed us to comfort and support them and to be patient.

But there is another class, the chronic seekers who, times without number, come to the penitent form, who seem to be tramping forever on an endless treadmill, who are with us and need wise and patient help as much or more than any other class of people. They have been to the penitent form so often that many have lost interest in them and have but little, if any, hope for them. But they are a challenge to our faith, love, pity, patience, spiritual intelligence, and resourcefulness. We must not let them perish in full view, and we must not let them slip away from view and perish in the night. They belong to us. They are our charge, and, if possible, we must win them and lead them into a joyful experience of salvation and perfect love. We need to take ourselves in hand in dealing with them, for possibly their failure is an evidence of our weakness of faith; our lack of burning, compassionate zeal; or of our spiritual and mental ignorance, poverty, and laziness.

We need to do some sober, hard thinking, some real praying, and "stir up the gift of God" within us (2 Tim. 1:6 KJV) if we are to fathom their deep needs and help them. Personally, I fear that in many instances it is the faulty, hasty way they are dealt with in prayer that accounts in part, if not wholly, for their miserable failures. "A curse on anyone who is lax in doing the LORD's work!" wrote Jeremiah (Jer. 48:10 NIV).

A thousand times I have trembled for seekers as I have seen people dealing with them who I have feared needed help themselves. Solomon said, "He who wins souls is wise" (Prov. 11:30 NKJV).

In the old days, when my hearing was more acute, I seldom let anyone leave the penitent form without dealing with the person myself. It was a great tax upon my time and strength, but my heart would not rest in peace until I had done my utmost to lead each one into light and into the sweet and assured rest of faith.

I felt I must make full proof of my ministry, and I measured its acceptance with God, and its harmony with His truth and His principles and Spirit, by its fruits in joyously saved and sanctified souls.

I once conducted meetings in a splendid city in which the territorial headquarters of The Salvation Army for that country is located. In it are many flourishing corps (churches) and service centers which command the respect and high regard of the citizens of both high and low degree.

In two corps in residential sections of that city, I conducted meetings that were well attended and in which people responded promptly to my invitations. Then I went downtown to the corps at the territorial headquarters. There, too, the crowds were large and attentive, but it was next to impossible to get anyone to the penitent form except as a result of the most dogged personal dealing and persuasion. To me this was a sore disappointment, for I always feel that if I preach the truth in love, luminously, pointedly, persuasively, with constant reliance upon the Holy Spirit, the people will promptly yield to my invitations, and if they do not do so, I feel the trouble must be with my spirit or manner of preaching.

I had been to this corps on two different occasions before, and the people seemed much more responsive at that time. I wondered at the present hardness.

After I had preached and poured out my heart upon the people, prayer warriors promptly began to "fish,"[3] but it was only after long effort that they would lead anyone to the penitent form. This continued for several meetings, and I was greatly perplexed. I noticed that those who came did not seem to be broken in spirit. There were no tears, but neither was there any levity. Usually there was a hard, set look on the faces of those who came, which seemed to say, "Well, if I must, I will, but I feel it is useless to come. Nothing will happen."

I noted further that as soon as anyone knelt at the penitent form someone would rush to his or her side, enter into conversation, and in a few minutes look up and say that he or she was all right. The seeker then would rise up with the same hard, set expression and take a seat. There was no tear in the eye, no light on the face, nothing that indicated that he or she had met with Jesus and found a great deliverance and peace.

On inquiry I found that most of those who were coming to the penitent form were well-known to the local leaders and had been forward again and again.

Loud music and singing in the prayer meeting may keep up a lively interest, but they sadly interfere with my hearing, so that it is most difficult for me to deal with seekers. I tried to find out how these people at the penitent form were being dealt with, and I discovered that they were usually asked one or two questions, told to obey God and trust, asked if they would do so, and when they said they would they were sent to their seat, as dead and hopeless, apparently, as when they came.

In some instances where their weaknesses and failures were well known they were dealt with in a severe, unsympathetic way that seemed to me anything but helpful, and quite unbecoming from any who felt that they themselves had been hewn from the rock and lifted out of miry clay. Sinners saved by grace must be careful how they deal with fellow sinners, lest, like Moses, they find that they have displeased the Lord.

Finally, a member of that corps came to the penitent form and not only threw himself down on his knees, but fell upon it in a way that seemed to me to indicate hopelessness. I took my Bible and knelt beside him, and I soon found out that he had come there again and again, that his trouble was fleshly sin, that he loathed himself, but that he felt powerless when temptation was upon him. He was eager to break away from his sin, but felt that he was its servant (see John 8:34; Rom. 6:16), its bond slave, and it mocked his struggles and good resolutions to quit it and be free. I felt, I saw, that hitherto he had been led to make resolutions and promises and told to trust in Christ, but that he had never been made to really see Christ as his Lord, his Redeemer, his Savior, who was down with him on his battlefield. I felt I must make him see this, and to this I set myself with prayer and full purpose of heart.

I told him he had been trusting in the strength of his own resolutions, in which there is no strength, and that he would surely fall again unless he found the Lord. We "are kept by the power of God through faith" (1 Pet. 1:5 KJV). Faith is the coupler that links us to God and His power. If the link fails, the power cannot operate in us. We must believe, and keep on believing, if we are to be kept. He saw it. He felt he must have God's power, God's presence, or he would fall again and fall forevermore. When I was assured that he realized this, I then opened my Bible and said to him, "You have made promises to God, now let us see what promises God makes to you." And we read together, "God demonstrates His own love toward us, in that while we were still sinners, Christ died for us" (Rom. 5:8 NKJV); "Where sin abounded, grace did much more abound" (Rom. 5:20 KJV); "Sin shall not have dominion over you, for you are not under law but under grace" (Rom. 6:14 NKJV); and "If we confess our sins, he is faithful and just to forgive us our sins, and to cleanse us from all unrighteousness" (1 John 1:9 KJV).

In these promises, he saw God's love for him in spite of his sin, and his face began to brighten. And, no longer lolling over the penitent form hopeless and seemingly as spineless as a jellyfish, he began to straighten up. It was as though a new backbone were entering into him.

Then I sought to show him how God promises to enter the battle with him against his sins and mocking, gripping habits, and we read, "Fear not, for I am with you" (Isa. 41:10 NKJV).

I asked him, "You have been afraid, haven't you—afraid you would fall? You are afraid now, are you not?"

"Oh, yes!" he replied. "I have been afraid, and I am now afraid."

"But listen: 'Fear not, for I am with you.' This is God's promise to you, my brother. He says, 'I am with you.' Do you not see that you are not alone? He is on the battlefield. He is in the thick of the fight with you. In the darkness of the night, in the glare of the day, when alone or in the throng, He is with you. Do you not see it? Will you, do you, believe it?"

And he began to see.

I kept reading. "'Be not dismayed.' When temptation assails you, when the enemy comes mocking and threatening, you are not alone, my brother. 'Be not dismayed, for I am your God' [Isa. 41:10 NKJV]. He is your God. Call upon Him, trust Him, and laugh at your foe in the name of the Lord, as the stripling David laughed at and defied Goliath. 'I will strengthen you.' Hitherto you have fallen because you were weak, but see, read it, believe it, God says, 'I will strengthen you, Yes, I will help you' [Isa. 41:10 NKJV].

"You wouldn't fall into your shameful sin if some strong, true, trusted friend were by your side, would you? And note, God is with you! And He says He will help you. Away with your fears!

"'I will uphold you with My righteous right hand' [Isa. 41:10 NKJV].

"Will you trust him? Will you cast to the winds your fears and henceforth go into every battle believing that God is with you, that almighty strength is pledged to you, that help is at hand, and that you shall be upheld? Will you lift your eyes to the Lord and trust instead of trembling and quailing when the enemies of your soul assail you?"

It was a joy to see my man. He looked; he read. Light burst upon him and beamed in his face. He seemed to be looking into the face of God.

He straightened up. "I see, oh, I see! I will, I do trust him!" And with thanksgiving he arose in the Spirit's power, and through the remainder of that campaign he was radiant. I trust he so remains to this day, and so he does if he obediently, believingly fights with the "sword of the Spirit, which is the word of God" (Eph. 6:17 KJV).

He saw the face of his divine Kinsman-Redeemer and heard the voice of the everlasting Father in the Word, and life and power and joy and peace flowed into him as he believed.

The Bible is the indispensable aid to faith. How do we get acquainted with God? By the work of the Holy Spirit in our minds and hearts as we penitently, obediently believe. But what are we to believe? We are to believe what He has said: "These things have I spoken unto you, that my joy might remain in you, and that your joy might be full," said Jesus (John 15:11 KJV).

"His divine power has granted to us all things that pertain to life and godliness, through the knowledge of him who called us to his own glory and excellence, by which he has granted to us his precious and very great promises, so that through them you may become partakers of the divine nature, having escaped from the corruption that is in the world because of sinful desire" (2 Pet. 1:3–4 ESV).

If we want to be strong, we must live "by every word that comes from the mouth of God" said Jesus (Matt. 4:4 ESV), as the Devil fiercely attacked Him.

"And as he spoke to me," said Daniel, "I was strengthened and said, 'Let my lord speak, for you have strengthened me'" (Dan. 10:19 ESV). And how was he strengthened? By the revelation of God through His Word.

How is a little child quieted, assured, and filled with peace in the night? By the presence and word of father or mother. And so we are assured, and made strong, and "thoroughly equipped for every good work" (2 Tim. 3:17 NIV) through the Scripture that is inspired by God and then brought to our remembrance and applied to our need by the Holy Spirit as we believe. Let us feed our people with the sincere milk of the Word and they will "grow into a full experience of salvation" (1 Pet. 2:2 NLT) and not tremble before the face of any mocking foe, but one person shall chase a thousand and two shall put ten thousand to flight (see Deut. 32:30).

While others debate the inspiration of the Word, let us eat it, drink it, preach it, and live by it, and we shall live in the power of "an endless life" (Heb. 7:16 KJV). It is still, as in the days of Job and the psalmist, "sweeter also than honey and the honeycomb" (Ps. 19:10 KJV) to those who believe and obey it, and more to be desired than "necessary food" (Job 23:12 KJV).

Within that awful volume lies

The mystery of mysteries!

Happiest they of human race

To whom God has granted grace

To read, to fear, to hope, to pray,

To lift the latch and force the way;

And better had they ne'er been born,

Who read to doubt, or read to scorn.[4]

So wrote Sir Walter Scott. And when dying he said to his son-in-law, "Bring me the Book."

"Which one, sir?" asked the son-in-law.

"There is but one," replied the dying man. "Bring me the Bible."[5]

## NOTES

1. Robert Browning, *The Poems of Robert Browning*, "Christmas Eve," part 20, lines 52–53 (London: Wordsworth Editions, 1994), 408.

2. Dwight L. Moody, quoted in *The Current* 2, no. 44 (October 18, 1884).

3. A practice of prayerfully discerning and approaching people who seem to be ready to respond to the Holy Spirit's prompting but may need encouragement to do so.

4. Sir Walter Scott, *The Monastery* (Edinburgh: Adam and Charles Black, 1853), 129.

5. Dean F. W. Farrar, *The Church of England Pulpit and Ecclesiastical Review*, vol. 41 (London: Church of England Pulpit Office, 1896), 291.

# *Whom Do You Trust?* 12

An exceptionally bright young woman wrote to me in a recent letter, "I have had experience enough to know that feelings do not count for much, and I do know that deep down in my heart there is a peace and sense of security that were not there when I was at your meetings last week. But I feel that my sense of security and faith are waiting to be tried before I can be quite sure of myself."

In those words are revealed a halting and mixed faith and a subtle temptation of the old Accuser.

Of course, our "faith and sense of security" are always being tried, and we should not ignore but quietly and confidently welcome such trial, for it is by the trial of faith that patience with the long and often stern disciplines of life is wrought in us and our character is perfected. James, in the second verse of his epistle, began with this common experience, saying, "Consider it pure joy, my brothers and sisters, whenever you face trials of many kinds, because you know that the testing of your faith produces perseverance. Let perseverance finish its work so that you may be mature and complete, not lacking anything" (James 1:2–4 NIV).

James got happy over this and exhorted his brothers and sisters to "consider it pure joy" to be tried. Not that the trial itself is pleasant, but the result is glorious. And Peter told us that in the midst of our rejoicing over present salvation through faith, we may be, "for a little while, if need be, grieved by various trials, that the genuineness of [our] faith, being much more precious than gold that perishes, though it is tested by fire, may be found to praise, honor, and glory at the revelation of Jesus Christ" (1 Pet. 1:6–7 NKJV).

So that young woman's feeling that her "faith and sense of security" will be tried is reasonable and normal, but her phrase—"before I can be quite sure of myself"—reveals a halting and mixed faith and the work of the subtle Tempter. He is slyly turning her eyes and her faith from Jesus to herself. "You can't be sure of yourself," he whispers, and almost imperceptibly she looks at self instead of to Jesus.

We are never to be sure of ourselves, but quietly, unwaveringly sure of our Redeemer and Lord. We shall be tried, but we shall not be left alone. As He was with the three young men in Nebuchadnezzar's seven-fold heated furnace, so He will be with us (see Dan. 3:24–25). "I am with you. . . . I am your God. I will strengthen you. . . . I will hold you up" (Isa. 41:10 NLT) is His ringing assurance. "I will never leave you nor forsake you" (Heb. 13:5 ESV). "No temptation has overtaken you that is not common to man. God is faithful, and he will not let you be tempted beyond your ability, but with the temptation he will also provide the way of escape, that you may be able to endure it" (1 Cor. 10:13 ESV).

Our blessed Lord Himself in the days of His flesh "faced all of the same testings we do," so He "understands our weaknesses" (Heb. 4:15 NLT), and is "able to help us" when we are tempted (Heb. 2:18 NLT). And He will help us if—instead of looking to ourselves and trembling in the presence of the mocking Enemy, with his army of fears and doubts—we look courageously and humbly, in the name of Jesus, to our Father who is the Lord God of hosts.

We are to face our fears in His name and rout our Enemy by an appeal to the all-sufficient merits of the blood shed for us, by glad testimony, and by a consecration that welcomes death rather than doubt and denial (see Rev. 12:10–11).

"Our God whom we serve is able to deliver us and he will," said Shadrach, Meshach, and Abednego. "But if not, be it known to you, O king, that we will not serve your gods or worship the golden image that you have set up" (Dan. 3:17–18 ESV). We will burn, but we will not bow. "They loved not their lives unto the death" (Rev. 12:11 KJV). That is consecration, and that is a firm basis for unwavering faith. They were not trusting in themselves, but in the living God, and deliverance came.

It is the Enemy of all souls who tempts us to look forward fearfully to some wholly indefinite trial that may never come, before we can walk in confident peace. Trials may come—they *will* come—but our Lord will be there with abundant grace when they do come if, moment by moment looking unto Him, we go forward in His strength.

It is one of the "wiles of the devil" (Eph. 6:11 KJV) to haunt us with nameless, shadowy fears of tomorrow. It is his way to weaken faith and turn our eyes from our Lord.

They may come, and they may not, but whether they come or not, we are not alone, and we must not fear, though the temptation to fear may be present.

Battle-hardened, mocking Goliath said to David, "Come to me, and I will give your flesh to the birds of the air and to the beasts of the field."

David answered, "You come to me with a sword and with a spear and with a javelin, but I come to you in the name of the LORD of hosts, the God of the armies of Israel, whom you have defied. This day the LORD will deliver you into my hand, and I will strike you down and cut off your head" (1 Sam. 17:44–46 ESV). The Lord was David's shield. He kept the Lord in front of him. "I have set the LORD always before me" (Ps. 16:8 KJV), David wrote long years after, and Goliath could not reach him without first encountering the Lord. And when the Philistine champion drew closer to meet David, the lad ran to meet him and defeated him in the name of the Lord.

That is the way to face fears and spiritual enemies and doubts and temptations. Face them "in the name of the LORD of hosts." Run to meet them, but put no confidence in yourself, only as you are "strong in the Lord, and in the power of his might" (Eph. 6:10 KJV).

Paul knew, as few others, what trouble and danger are. He said, "The Holy Spirit testifies to me in every city that imprisonment and afflictions await me." But, he added, "I do not account my life of any value nor as precious to myself, if only I may finish my course and the ministry that I received from the Lord Jesus" (Acts 20:23–24 ESV).

And again he wrote, "I am sure that neither death nor life, nor angels nor rulers, nor things present nor things to come, nor powers, nor height nor depth, nor anything else in all creation, will be able to separate us from the love of God in Christ Jesus our Lord" (Rom. 8:38–39 ESV). His confidence was wholly in the changeless character and love of his Lord, therefore he trembled in the presence of no one, nor any combination of trials that might overtake him.

# *A Word to Those*
# *Who Are Growing Old* **13**

In one of my recent meetings, a dear sister, who has been serving the Lord and walking in the light for many years, confessed with tears that her joy was not what it used to be. In her youth, joy was rapturous, leaping up like springing fountains and singing birds. A verse of Scripture would suddenly stand out with its assuring message and fill her with gladness, and songs in the night welled up from her glad heart, but now she says she often has heaviness of spirit, and the way seems to get harder. And while she feels sure that she is accepted by God, yet she is not enjoying what she once enjoyed.

God forbid that I should offer any false comfort or, through lack of faith, limit His power to fill us with the rapturous joys of youth as we grow older. But is it reasonable for us to suppose that this should be so? In youth as we waited upon the Lord we found our spiritual strength renewed, and we mounted up "with wings as eagles." In middle age, as we wait upon the Lord, we find our strength renewed and we "run and [are not] weary." In old age, as we wait upon the Lord, our strength is renewed, but we must now "walk, and not faint" (Isa. 40:31 KJV).

None of the natural senses are as keen in old age as in youth. The appetite for food, the joy in society, and the rapturous friendships of youth do not continue quite the same through the years. And may it not be so spiritually? It is true that the apostle said while "outwardly we are wasting away, yet inwardly we are being renewed day by day" (2 Cor. 4:16 NIV). But is not the joy—in some measure, at least—modified by the sobering experiences of the years? The river that started as a bubbling, leaping, laughing brook in the mountains, often rushing in torrents through narrow and precipitous ways, gradually widens and deepens and flows peacefully and without noise as it nears the sea. May it not be so in our spiritual life? Is not the river of God's peace flowing through the hearts of the aged a deeper and richer experience than the exuberant joys at the beginning of the spiritual life?

The pressing infirmities of the flesh, and the gradual decay of memory and other powers, may account for some of the apparent loss of joy in those who are growing old.

The enlarged knowledge of the malignant, massive, stubborn powers of evil may have a sobering effect upon the mind that, if not watchfully guarded against and met with quiet, steadfast faith, may tend to lessen joy.

If our children do not serve God with the ardor we wish, or souls for whom we pray do not at once experience new life in Christ, or the work of God that is dear to our hearts languishes, the Devil may tempt us to doubt or repine, and so our joy is quenched.

What steps can be taken to prevent or arrest the failure of joy?

Older people should still stir up the gift of God that is in them as we stir up a fire that is burning low. Frequent seasons of prayer, along with singing and humming through old songs, with an active exercise of faith, will help to keep the joy bells ringing. I am a rather poor sleeper, and recently in the small hours of the night, before the birds were singing, I found myself wide awake. So, to bless my own soul and control and guide my thoughts without disturbing others, I softly sang, in almost a whisper, "I Need Thee, Oh, I Need Thee," and my heart was strangely warmed and blessed as I sang.

Older people are not wise to spend too much time considering the joys of long ago and comparing them with present emotions. They should live in anticipation of joys yet to come rather than dwell upon joys that are past. God's storehouse is not exhausted. For those who love and follow Jesus, "the best is yet to be."[1] Paul said that he forgot the things that were behind and, looking forward, pressed like an eager racer toward the things that were ahead (see Phil. 3:13–14).

Those who keep looking backward instead of forward are likely to stumble and miss the joys that spring up round about them. It is not good to be comparing the present with the past, but we should each moment seek to exercise full and glad faith in our Lord for the present and the future. He has a portion of joy for us now. But the ineffable glory and blessing and joy are yet to come, when we see Him face-to-face and hear Him say, "Well done; come!"

We must keep our eyes on Jesus, looking unto Him, the Author and the Finisher of our faith (see Heb. 12:2). We must look away from the seen things to unseen, eternal things; to the purpose and covenant of God in Christ, steadfast and sure; to His promises, great and precious, shining like stars forever and assuring us of God's interest in us.

We should carefully count up our present mercies and blessings and give thanks for them. It may be better with us than we think. John Fletcher said that he at one time became so eager for what he had not yet received that he failed to rejoice and enjoy the things God had already given him. That is an almost certain way to lose what we have. It is good—indeed, it is a duty—to stretch out for the things ahead, but we must not forget to give God thanks and enjoy the things He gives us now.

In feeble health, we may not be able to realize all we have to be glad about. There may at times be deep and prolonged depression of spirit arising from physical causes. "The body and soul are near neighbors," said the founder of The Salvation Army, William Booth, "and they greatly influence each other." Elijah was physically exhausted when he got under that juniper tree and wanted to die, but God let him sleep, awakened him, gave him a simple meal of bread and water, let him sleep again, awakened and fed him again and let him live in the open, in sunshine and fresh air, and so revived him, gave him a man's work to do, and took him to heaven in a chariot of fire. All God's resources were not exhausted because Elijah was depressed and exhausted. The best was yet to be with Elijah! Simple food, fresh air, sunshine, labor, and rest are still important for old people, if they wish to keep a happy experience.

Finally, older people should still go to the house of God and mingle with God's people. It was in the temple that aged Simeon and Anna the prophetess found the little Lord Jesus. And the psalmist sang, if not from his own experience, then from observation of others and in assured faith, "Those who are planted in the house of the LORD shall flourish in the courts of our God. They shall still bear fruit in old age; they shall be fresh and flourishing, to declare that the LORD is upright" (Ps. 92:13–15 NKJV).

> When darkness seems to veil His face,
> I rest on His unchanging grace . . .
> I dare not trust the sweetest frame
> But wholly lean on Jesus' name.[2]

## NOTES

1. Robert Browning, "Rabbi Ben Ezra," *Poems of Robert Browning* (London: Oxford University Press, 1923), 636–638.

2. Edward Mote, "My Hope Is Built on Nothing Less," 1834, public domain.

# *Answering Atheism* 14

A wide knowledge of history tends to sanity, sobriety, and correctness of judgment of people and events, if we have seen God in history. We need such knowledge to give us perspective, to steady us, to save us from sharp judgments, and to insure us against cockiness on one hand and despair on the other. Without this wide, long view, we are like a tiny boat on a tempestuous sea, tossed on the waves, but with it we are more like a great ship that rides serenely over the billows.

To the casual observer the experience of humanity seems tidal—always flowing and ebbing like the tides of the sea—or forever moving in a circle, getting nowhere, evermore coming back from whence it started, like the rivers rising out of and returning to the sea. To such a person the "one far-off divine event, to which the whole creation moves,"[1] the slow but sure workings of Providence, and the unfailing purpose and process of the divine government are hidden.

When I was a child on the wide, bare, unprotected prairies of the American Midwest, black clouds and fierce thunderstorms filled me with anxious fears and vague terror. But as I grew to manhood, I saw them as a part of a vast and ordered whole, and they lost their power to create panic in me.

Once, when sick and prostrated in health, I was thrown into a state of mental and spiritual anxiety, amounting almost to torture, by the nationwide excitement over a great prizefight. I felt our American civilization was only veneered barbarism, and for a time it seemed to me that we were reverting to, and were to be swallowed up by, brutal, sensuous paganism. Then, on my knees praying, I remembered the days when a thousand gladiators fought each other to the death in the Coliseum, or battled and struggled with and were devoured by wild beasts to make a Roman holiday, while the mobs of the city by the hundred thousand, headed by the emperor, senators, philosophers, noble ladies, and all the elite gloated over the cruel, bloody scene. Then in deep reverence, gratitude, and glad trust I gave God thanks, as I saw how far He had led us on—and was still leading—from those ghastly pleasures, those merciless days.

When I was a child, the American Civil War was raging. Soldiers marched and countermarched through our peaceful little valley and village. Armies stormed and thundered across the land. Proud cities were besieged and starved and fell before conquering hosts. Fathers, brothers, and sons were perishing in bloody combat, in fetid swamps and prison camps. Homes were vanishing. Funeral bells were ever tolling. Mothers, sisters, wives, and orphans were ever weeping. The foundations of the social order seemed to be crumbling, and people turned their thoughts to the apocalyptic portions of Scripture, tried to interpret the times by their symbolisms, and turned their eyes to the clouds in expectation of the Savior's bodily appearing, longing for Him to come and work out the salvation which men and women—abasing their pride and yielding to the lordship of Jesus, under the leadership of the sanctifying Spirit—must work out for themselves, or perish. It was years before the light of history enabled me to escape this bald interpretation of apocalyptic symbols and walk in quietness and peace and close attention to daily duty, while a world quaked and trembled in unparalleled hurricanes of war, assured that "the heavens do rule" (Dan. 4:26 KJV), and "a watcher and an holy one" (Dan. 4:23 KJV) in the heavens was interested in our perplexity and sore travail and would guide us through the storm and tempest, purified and chastened, to a haven of peace.

History is repeating itself in spirit among us, and a society—a very militant society—for the propagation of atheism has recently received letters of incorporation from the legislators of New York, and an anti-Bible society has also been incorporated. Its avowed object is "to discredit the Bible," to "make known its human origin, evolutionary formation, and its discreditable history; expose its immoral and barbaric contents; and lay bare its antiscientific, antiliberal, and irrational teachings." Such is its program. It proposes to show that "the Bible is the work of man." It claims that the "falsification by deliberate mistranslation is the sole basis of orthodoxy." It promises that "the inhuman character of the Bible—God—shall be offered in evidence against the Book," and "the Bible patriarchs shall be shown to be a set of unmatched moral monsters." It continues, saying, "The spirit of injustice and intolerance dominate the Bible," "the Sermon on the Mount consists mainly of romantic sentimentalism unrelated to reality," and "the Bible is inimical to civilization. It must and shall be discredited." It urges, "The American Anti-Bible Society has no religious tests for membership, except disbelief in the Bible as divinely inspired. . . . Help us free America from Bible-bondage."

Those are some tidbits from its bulletin or manifesto. The Society for the Propagation of Atheism has already enlisted many young people and students, and societies of "damned souls" (as they dub themselves) are flourishing in many of our schools and colleges. It is all a part of a nationwide, worldwide movement, awash of wide, sweeping waves of atheism gushing forth from the heart of the Russian Revolution, something that all lovers of our Lord and of the Bible will have to face and possibly come into close and desperate grips with in the near future.

If these people were better acquainted with history, they might not be so cocksure of discrediting the Bible and banishing God from His throne. If we are acquainted with history, we shall not be uncertain as to the final issue, but neither will we sit down in a fool's paradise and think we can drive back the waves of mocking, irresponsible, desperate unbelief by witty retort, smart rejoinder, or learned and masterly debate.

How shall we reply to their denial of the divine elements of the Bible? How shall we prove it to be God-inspired? Is it a subject of proof or of faith? How can I be sure of it for myself, and how can I prove it to others? Paul said, "All Scripture is given by inspiration of God" (2 Tim. 3:16 KJV) but that is an assertion, not a proof. It still has to be proved, if it can be.

I had studied the various arguments for the inspiration of the Bible by theologians, and since I had from my infancy onward accepted the Bible as God's Book, they confirmed my unquestioning faith. But there came a time when I needed more than learned arguments to prove it to me. And not until God Himself came to my help was I wholly, invincibly convinced.

That which finally established my faith in the divinity of the Bible was opened eyes, an inner illumination of my own soul which enabled me to behold wondrous things all through its sacred pages. "Open my eyes, that I may see wondrous things from Your law," prayed the psalmist (Ps. 119:18 NKJV). The Book is largely sealed to people with unanointed eyes and self-satisfied or world-satisfied hearts, and from those who turn from the paths of rectitude and "stumble because they are disobedient to the word" (1 Pet. 2:8 NASB).

The pastor of the church of Laodicea became lukewarm as a result of getting rich and increasing in goods until he felt he had need of nothing, but knew not that he was "wretched, and miserable, and poor, and blind, and naked" (Rev. 3:17 KJV).

"I advise you," Jesus said, "to buy from me gold made pure in fire so you can be truly rich. Buy from me white clothes so you can be clothed and so you can cover your shameful nakedness. Buy from me medicine to put on your eyes so you can truly see" (Rev. 3:18 NCV). The Book was sealed to the pastor, and the revelations of the Lord were hidden from him, because of the self-imposed blindness or dimness of his spiritual eyes.

The final blessing Jesus gave His disciples just before He ascended from them was the blessing of this inner illumination of opened eyes.

"Then he opened their minds to understand the Scriptures" (Luke 24:45 NLT).

The sun does not need learned astronomical treatises to prove its existence, nor a manmade candle to enable it to be seen. All it needs is that we should have eyes to see. It is its own evidence. What the sun is in the world of material things, the Bible is in the world of spiritual things. It carries in itself its evidences of inspiration. It is a lamp to the feet and a light to the path of those whose spiritual eyes are open and who will resolutely follow where it leads. Let us notice some of the assertions of the Book and find if they can be proven, not by argument but by life, by experience, for if it does not answer the deep needs of life, the hunger of the soul, the fears, the hopes, the aspirations, and the questionings of the human spirit, the Bible is merely a venerable and curious bit of ancient literature to be read for pleasure or to gratify curiosity.

"People do not live by bread alone," said Jesus, "but by every word that comes from the mouth of God" (Matt. 4:4 NLT). Does the Bible feed the human soul? All the saints and soldiers of Jesus through the ages have been nourished and have lived on the Word of God. "I have esteemed the words of his mouth more than my necessary food," said Job (Job 23:12 KJV). "How sweet your words taste to me; they are sweeter than honey," wrote the psalmist (Ps. 119:103 NLT). "They are more desirable than gold," sang David, "even the finest gold. They are sweeter than honey, even honey dripping from the comb" (Ps. 19:10 NLT). "Your words were found, and I ate them," said Jeremiah, "and your words became to me a joy and the delight of my heart" (Jer. 15:16 ESV).

Does the Bible help men and women to live finer, cleaner, saintly lives? It certainly does. Those who receive the Word of God into their hearts will stop sinning. "I have hidden your word in my heart that I might not sin against you" wrote the psalmist (Ps. 119:11 NIV). "How can a young person stay pure? By obeying your word" (Ps. 119:9 NLT).

Does the Bible offer hope to the soul who has scorned the voice of conscience and turned away from light and goodness and God? It is the only book in the world that does. It, and it alone, tells of a redeeming God, a Savior from sin, and a loving heavenly Father who waits to welcome sinners. "But God showed his great love for us by sending Christ to die for us while we were still sinners" (Rom. 5:8 NLT). "This is a trustworthy saying, and everyone should accept it: 'Christ Jesus came into the world to save sinners'" (1 Tim. 1:15 NLT). "If we confess our sins, he is faithful and just to forgive us our sins, and to cleanse us from all unrighteousness" (1 John 1:9 KJV). Ten thousand times ten thousand sinners saved by faith in the Savior revealed in the Bible will testify to the truth of those words.

Does the Bible offer aid to tempted men and women? Does it comprehend our need? It does as no other book in the world does. It reveals an elder Brother who helps us overcome our temptations. "For because he himself has suffered when tempted, he is able to help those who are being tempted" (Heb. 2:18 ESV). "This High Priest of ours understands our weaknesses, for he faced all of the same testings we do, yet he did not sin" (Heb. 4:15 NLT). "God is faithful, and he will not let you be tempted beyond your ability, but with the temptation he will also provide the way of escape, that you may be able to endure it" (1 Cor. 10:13 ESV).

Does the Bible have any word for the burdened, perplexed, and careworn? It does, sweet words of comprehension and assurance that can be found nowhere else: "Come to me, all who labor and are heavy laden, and I will give you rest" (Matt. 11:28 ESV).

Has the Bible any word for the persecuted, maligned, and oppressed? Listen: "Blessed are those who are persecuted for righteousness' sake, for theirs is the kingdom of heaven. Blessed are you when others revile you and persecute you and utter all kinds of evil against you falsely on my account. Rejoice and be glad, for your reward is great in heaven" (Matt. 5:10–12 ESV).

Has it any word for the oppressed and afflicted? Listen: "He has not ignored or belittled the suffering of the needy. He has not turned his back on them, but has listened to their cries for help" (Ps. 22:24 NLT). "If we suffer we shall also reign with him" (2 Tim. 2:12 KJV). "For our light affliction, which is but for a moment, is working for us a far more exceeding and eternal weight of glory" (2 Cor. 4:17 NKJV).

Has the Bible a word for those whose eyes are dim with tears? "God will wipe away every tear from their eyes" (Rev. 7:17 ESV).

For those who are in pain? "Neither shall there be mourning, nor crying, nor pain anymore" (Rev. 21:4 ESV).

Has it any word about the far future? "What we will be has not yet appeared; but we know that when he appears we shall be like him, because we shall see him as he is" (1 John 3:2 ESV).

How can I prove the inspiration of the Bible?

1. By the way it answers to the human heart. The key that fits an intricate lock was evidently made for that lock. The Bible meets me at every point of my moral and spiritual need. It fits my heart's intricate

needs as the key fits the lock. And I exult to know that the divine hand that fashioned me gives me the Book, and His heart that loves me pours itself with fathomless comforts into my heart through the Book. But I cannot prove to you the truth of the Book any more than I can prove that the sun is shining, that honey is sweet, that the song of the bird is melodious. The inspiration of the Bible is proved by experience, not by logic. "Meditate on it day and night" (Josh. 1:8 ESV), and you shall taste its sweetness, behold its wonders, and hear in its words the whisperings of the everlasting Father to the heart of His child.

2. By the evidence of a redeemed life. How shall I prove to others—to those who question, doubt, and deny—that the Bible is a God-given, God-inspired Book? Shall I go to history, science, or archaeology for proof? Yes, at the proper time and to the right people. But the most convincing proof of the inspiration of the Bible I can offer to an unbeliever is a redeemed life, lived in the power and sweetness of the Spirit; a life that matches the Bible; a life of love, prayer, faith, and devotion; a life of joy and peace and patience and sweet goodwill to all; a life full of good works matching a glad testimony to the saving, sanctifying, keeping power and ever-living presence of the Lord Jesus; a life like that of a Chinese Christian whose neighbors said of him, "There is no difference between him and the Book." He was a living Bible known and read by them all, and they saw and felt its truth in him. He was inbreathed, indwelt of God, and through him they recognized inspiration in the Book. Redeemed lives, drawing light and strength and inspiration from and matching the inspired Book, are the unanswerable proofs of its inspiration.

Sir Wilfred Grenfell of Labrador said that when he was a university student in England he lived with a professor who was a lecturer on the evidences of Christianity. This lecturer was in frequent controversy with skeptics, but never won over any of them. They would meet in public debate, each supported by his friends and followers, who were confirmed in their opinions, but there was no changing of sides and no one became a follower of Jesus. It was heady, a rivalry of wits, a struggle for mastery, an intellectual fisticuffs to no profit. But one day one of the most formidable of these skeptic debaters was stricken with a fatal illness. His friends had no words of comfort and left him to himself. Then a sweet, humble Salvation Army sister stepped in and nursed the dying man. She could not and did not argue with him, but revealed to him a redeemed, Christlike life. Love was in her face, tenderness was in her touch, grace was on her lips, and peace and joy in Jesus radiated from her. Soon, a humble, inspired life did what knowledge and argument had failed to do. He surrendered his life to Jesus Christ and died in the faith.

A skeptic challenged a man of God to debate about religion. "I accept your challenge on this condition," replied the man of God, "that I bring one hundred men with me to testify what faith in Christ has done for them, and you bring one hundred men to testify what atheism has done for them." The challenger withdrew the challenge, and there was no debate.

Meek and lowly, but glad and bold witnesses, who witness by lip and life and shining look, are the strongest argument for the faith they live. The final proof will be given when the risen Jesus appears with crowns and thrones and kingdoms and honor and glory and immortality for those who have believed and loved and followed Him to the end, and opens the dark gates of doom and banishes into "wrath and

fury . . . tribulation and distress . . . every human being who does evil"
(Rom. 2:8–9 ESV).

## NOTE

1. Alfred Lord Tennyson, "In Memoriam," n. d., public domain.

# *The Lord's Own Prayer* 15

One day, at a certain place we are told, the disciples were with Jesus when He was praying, and after He had ceased—I wonder how long He prayed and what was the burden of His prayer?—one of His disciples said to Him, "Lord, teach us to pray, as John also taught his disciples" (Luke 11:1 KJV). He did not say teach us *how* to pray, but teach us to pray. It was not the manner of praying he desired to be taught, but simply to pray. And this Jesus did, both by what He said and even more by what He did, by His example. They often found Him praying, and that taught them to pray as no words or exhortations could teach them. However, Jesus responded to this request and taught them a prayer that, wherever it is known at all, is known as "The Lord's Prayer."

But it is rather the *disciples'* prayer. It is a prayer He gave *them* to use, voicing their needs and their desires.

The *Lord's* Prayer—the prayer Jesus as our Great High Priest addressed to the Father; the prayer in which He poured out the desires of His heart for the Father's glory and His fellowship in that glory and in which He voiced His longings for the disciples then with Him, and for us and for all who would believe in Him; the prayer which no doubt constitutes the substance of His ceaseless and eternal intercession for His disciples of all time and everywhere—is recorded in John 17. That is more appropriately called "The Lord's Prayer."

Jesus had said to Mary at the wedding in Cana, when she told Him of the empty wine vessels, "Woman, what does this have to do with me? My hour has not yet come" (John 2:4 ESV). To His brothers who were skeptical of His claims, and who would hasten Him to Jerusalem, there either to prove or discredit Himself, He said, "My time has not yet come, but your time is always here. . . . You go up to the feast. I am not going up to this feast, for my time has not yet fully come" (John 7:6, 8 ESV). Once the religious authorities were angered at Jesus. John explained that at that point "no one arrested him, because his hour had not yet come" (John 8:20 ESV).

But finally, when Jesus' ceaseless but unhasting ministry was drawing to a close, and He had come up to Jerusalem for the last time, Greek worshipers said to Philip, "Sir, we would see Jesus." When this was told to Jesus, He answered, "The hour is come" (John 12:21, 23 KJV).

Then, with His disciples, He went into the upper room and ate the Passover Feast, ate of the Paschal Lamb, which ever since that dread night when the destroying angel passed over Egypt had pointed in type to Him, the great antitype, God's Lamb, whose blood would cleanse from all sin and shelter from the Destroyer all who believed.

After supper He arose, girded Himself, and washed the disciples' feet, showing them by a kindergarten lesson what, through their dullness and hardness of heart, His words had failed to teach them: that He who would be greatest among them must be, and would gladly be, "servant of all" (Mark 10:44 KJV).

After this object lesson in lowly, loving service, He spoke tender words to them, words of warning, comfort, command, instruction, and encouragement. He unfolded to them the person and mission of the "other Comforter," who would come to them when He was gone. He assured them that while He was going away, He would come again; He would not leave them comfortless or orphans. While absent in body, He would yet be present in Spirit. If they but loved Him and kept His commandment to love one another, they would have with them evermore His manifested presence, His spiritual presence, in their hearts and minds, made possible and real through simple, obedient faith; they would be loved by the Father, and He and the Father would come to make Their abode, Their mansion, with them and in them. His joy would be in them, and their joy would be full. He warned them that the world would hate them because it hated Him, and because they were His friends and not of the world. He told them they would be persecuted and have sorrow, but added, "Your grief will suddenly turn to wonderful joy. . . . Then you will rejoice, and no one can rob you of that joy. . . . Here on earth you will have many trials and sorrows. But take heart, because I have overcome the world" (John 16:20, 22–33 NLT).

They were to be so identified with Him, so "mixed up with Jesus," as a quaint old friend of mine once said, that His union with the Father and the love with which the Father loved Him—His joy, His tribulation, and His triumph and victory—would be theirs. They would share in all that was His. If they loved Him, trusted Him, bore His cross, and shared His sufferings, they would share His glory. If they labored and toiled with Him in tears, they would shout with Him at the ingathering of the sheaves and be jubilant in the harvest home. If they sorrowed with Him, they would also rejoice with Him. He was going to prepare a place for them, and He would come again and receive them that they might be where He was. He would not be in heaven and leave them behind.

It was His farewell address, recorded by John in chapters 13 to 16. It was the final lecture and tender, searching charge to these cadets of His own choice and training, who were soon to be commissioned and sent forth to conquer a hostile world by their testimony and sacrificial devotion and love, and turn it upside down.

He had spoken at length to His humble disciples, and now He lifted His eyes to heaven and spoke to the Father. He prayed, and this He did as naturally and as familiarly as He had spoken to His lowly followers.

He said, "Father, the hour has come" (John 17:1 NLT)—the fateful hour for which He had girded Himself and waited, the hour to which without pause and without haste He had pressed forward, the hour to which He had looked from the beginning of His ministry, the hour to which He had looked from of old, from the dawn of time when the morning stars sang together, and the hour to which He had looked from the deeps of timeless eternity. It was the zero hour of the moral world, of the spiritual universe. The zero hour in the great battle for the souls of humanity, the hour when our Kinsman-Redeemer was to "go over the top," go over "alone: for of the people there was none with Him,"[1] go over and die, die for us, die that we might live and never die. It was the hour of His utter humiliation, when all His glory was stripped from Him and laid aside, and He who knew no sin was made sin for us, "numbered with the transgressors . . . wounded for our transgressions . . . bruised for our iniquities," chastened for our peace, and stricken that we might be healed (Isa. 53:12, 5 KJV).

Step-by-step He had descended from infinite heights of glory and honor and power to infinite depths of weakness and reproach and shame. He, the infinitely pure and innocent One, came and united Himself with us as a human being, stood in our place, and took upon Himself our guilt, our sin, our shame, our curse. He was "made a curse for us" (Gal. 3:13 KJV). He was "made . . . sin for us" (2 Cor. 5:21 KJV). He emptied Himself of His divine, eternal majesty and took "the form of a servant, being born in the likeness of men. And being found in human form, he humbled himself by becoming obedient to the point of death, even death on a cross" (Phil. 2:7–8 ESV). This was the hour to which He had looked, to which He had at last come, and for the agony, the loneliness, the shame of which He was then, and had been from the beginning, girding Himself.

But before the dread and awful stroke of this hour fell upon Him, His thoughts turned to His poor, ignorant, weak, imperfect disciples, and with a love that knew no bounds—that forgot self, forgot the shame and agony soon to be poured out upon Him without stint like an ocean flood, even forgot or for a time ignored the glory so soon to follow on His return to the bosom of the Father and the bliss of heaven—He remembered them and prayed for them.

If we wish to know His thought for us, the fullness of blessing He wishes to bestow upon us, the completeness and intimacy of the union into which He wishes to enter with us, and the intimacy of the union and fellowship we are to have with the Father; if we wish to know how His purposes of world conquest are to be accomplished; if we wish to know the high estate, the glory, to which He intends to lift us, we should ponder this prayer, make it a daily study, and cooperate with Him for its fulfillment. He was not then talking to His lowly disciples. He was not commanding and charging them. He was talking to the Father for them, voicing their needs, considering their dangers, pleading their weakness, and with supplications and intercessions seeking for them boundless blessings that would make them kings and priests unto God, lifting them infinitely above the paltry pomp and fading glory of all the kings and governors and mighty ones of earth.

And through them in answer to this prayer are to flow all the streams and rivers of His grace, and be accomplished all the redemptive purposes of His sacrificial life and death here upon earth, and His risen life and resurrection power revealed from heaven. He is the Vine, they are the branches. Through them His beauty is to be made manifest, the beauty of holiness. In them His fruit is to be found, the fruit of the Spirit, the fruit of the life that is eternal, the fruit which is "love, joy, peace, longsuffering, kindness, goodness, faithfulness, gentleness, self-control" and against which "there is no law" (Gal. 5:22–23 NKJV).

The petitions of this prayer are few. He first prays for Himself—that the Father will glorify Him that He in turn may glorify the Father, and that He may again be glorified with the glory that was His with the Father before the world existed. And this petition was heard and considered, and we see the beginning of the abundant answer when the angel strengthened Him during the agony and bloody sweat of the garden, after which, with lamb-like submission and serene, unfailing meekness and patience, He calmly faced the mockery and shame of Herod's soldiers and Pilate's judgment hall, and the deeper and final agony and desertion of the cross.

We see it further answered in His resurrection from the dead, whereby, wrote Paul, He was indubitably "declared to be the Son of God with power, according to the spirit of holiness, by the resurrection from the dead" (Rom. 1:4 KJV). And we see a yet further and fuller answer when on the day of Pentecost the Holy Spirit was outpoured in His name, and His lowly disciples became living flames of love and holiness and power divine. And we see the continuing answer to this petition in every triumph of the gospel, in every penitent soul born into the kingdom, in every child of God sanctified, in every hymn of praise sung, and in every true prayer offered in His name. We see it in the light of His cross shining across centuries and millennia and gradually irradiating the dark places of all life, and the spread of His gospel from that narrow little circle in Jerusalem to all the continents and isles of earth. And as He is glorified, so is the Father.

Then He prayed for His disciples, whom the Father has given and will give to Him—prayed that they may be kept from the evil that is in the world. While He was with them in the world He had kept them. "The LORD God is a sun and a shield" (Ps. 84:11 KJV). He had been their sun. He had lighted their way, and they had walked in His light and had not stumbled out of the way. He was their shield. He had defended them against wily men and yet more wily devils. No enemy had been able to pluck out of His hand any save Judas, who sold himself to the Evil One for a handful of silver.

But now Jesus was leaving them, and they would be exposed to the wiles of the Evil One, who would subtly approach them as an "angel of light" (2 Cor. 11:14 KJV), rush upon and assail them "as a roaring lion" (1 Pet. 5:8 KJV), and make battle against them like an ancient archer with fiery darts of accusation, doubts, fears, and perplexities. And they would be beset by the relentless hostility of the world. The bigotry and hate of others and the proud scorn and fierce persecutions of cruel and idolatrous nations would be poured out upon them. They were as sheep in the midst of wolves. Great and constant would be their danger, measureless would be their need; therefore He prayed, "Holy Father, keep through Your name those whom You have given Me, that they may be one as We are" (John 17:11 NKJV).

He did not pray that they may be caught up out of the world and away from the evil, but that in the midst of it they may be kept through His name. "May the name of the God of Jacob protect you," prayed the psalmist David (Ps. 20:1 ESV). "The name of the LORD is a strong fortress; the godly run to him and are safe," said Solomon (Prov. 18:10 NLT). "Jesus, Jesus, Jesus," moaned and cried a sorely tempted ex-drunkard, and at the name the spell of the temptation was broken and he was kept through that name.

They were His little, defenseless ones, very dear to Him, and He wanted them kept for their own sakes. But they were also His representatives. As the Father had sent Him into the world, so He was now sending them into the world. They went forth in His name, with His word, on His business, and only as they were kept would the purpose of His life and death be fulfilled.

To this end He further prayed, "Sanctify them" (John 17:17 KJV). Set them apart, consecrate them to Yourself and to Your service, seal them and make them holy. Not only "keep them from the evil that is in the world," but also save them from the evil and corruption that is in their own hearts. Make them clean. Refine them as with fire. Purify them until no spot of sin remains upon them, until they are "all glorious within" (Ps. 45:13 KJV). "Sanctify them by Your truth. Your word is truth" (John 17:17 NKJV). Let Your truth search them until they are wholly conformed to Your nature and Your will, until their lives match Your truth and in them the truth lives incarnate and walks the earth.

Not for these alone, however, did He pray, but for all who should through their word believe in Him. His thought was girdling the globe and embracing the ages. Wherever and whenever a penitent, trembling soul believed in Him through their word, that soul came within the desire and purpose of this prayer. He wanted them all to be one, bound up in one bundle of life, one as He and the Father are one, that they might be the habitation of God upon earth, and that the world seeing this might believe in Him. Faith in Him depended on the brotherly love and unity of His disciples. So it did, and so it does to this day. When there is unity, there is faith. Where there is division, there is doubt. Thousands believed and a multitude of priests were obedient to the faith after Pentecost when the disciples were filled with the Holy Spirit and were of one mind and heart. But when this unity of faith and love was lost, the Dark Ages followed, and darkness and unbelief always follow loss of love and unity.

"The glory which You gave Me I have given them, that they may be one just as We are one," said He (John 17:22 NKJV). The religion of Jesus is social. It is inclusive, not exclusive. We can have the glory only as we are united. We must be one in spirit with our brothers and sisters. Let division come, and the glory departs. Let the unity of brotherly love continue, and the glory abides. O, let us beware of the leakage of love, of the loss of the spirit of unity, of the subtlety and snare and death of the spirit of distrust and division.

"I in them, and You in Me; that they may be made perfect in one, and that the world may know that You have sent Me, and have loved them as You have loved Me" (John 17:23 NKJV). In this world the disciples of Jesus are God's home, and that home is to be filled with sweet accord, not discord. He wants us to be "perfect in one" (John 17:23 KJV). Then the world—the poor, proud, foolish, wicked world—shall not only believe, but know that Jesus was sent by the Father, and that the love of the Father is outpoured upon His disciples as it was upon Himself. What responsibility this places upon us to foster the unity of the Spirit, and to beware of the pride and jealousy and envy and suspicion and unholy spirit of lordship that leads to division. Let us be content to wash each other's feet and be ambitious only to be servants of all.

In conclusion He prayed, "Father, I desire that they also whom You gave Me may be with Me where I am, that they may behold My glory which You have given Me; for You loved Me before the foundation of the world" (John 17:24 NKJV). O my soul, you who have wandered in darkness and grubbed in sin and been plucked from the mire shall yet be lifted from the dunghill and seated with Him upon His throne, and shall stand amid the blinding splendor and behold the glory before which angels and archangels, cherubim and seraphim, veil their faces and fall as dead. Toil on, O my soul! If you labor for Him, you will also reap with Him. He is not unrighteous to forget your work and labor of love, and He will not fail to reward abundantly your patience of hope. "Your labor in the Lord is not in vain" (1 Cor. 15:58 NIV). If you are called to suffer with Him, O my soul, count it all joy. Do not repine. Fear not. Faint not. You shall reign with Him. He has so promised. And He will remember. He will not forget His own word upon which He has caused you to hope (see Ps. 119:49).

If you love Him who died for you, who entrusts His honor and His cause to you, prove your love, O my soul, by feeding and watching over His lambs and sheep. Love your brothers and sisters as He has loved you. And as He laid down His life for you so, if necessary, lay down your life for your brothers and sisters, and so shall everyone know that you are His disciple. And "when he sees all that is accomplished by his anguish, he will be satisfied" (Isa. 53:11 NLT).

O what wonder! How amazing!
Jesus, glorious King of Kings,
Deigns to call me His beloved,
Lets me rest beneath His wings!
All for Jesus, resting now beneath His wings.

All for Jesus, all for Jesus,

All my being's ransomed powers;

All my thoughts and words and doings,

All my days and all my hours.

All for Jesus, all my days and all my hours.[2]

And when the days and hours of time are no more, then eternity—eternity with Him, my Redeemer, Lover, Friend, in "the glory that excels" (2 Cor. 3:10 NKJV) and that has no end.

## NOTES

1. Adam Clarke, *Matthew to the Acts*, Clarke's Commentary, vol. 5 (New York: Abingdon-Cokesbury, n.d.), 496.

2. Mary D. James, "All for Jesus," 1871, public domain.

# The Care of Souls  16

Many years ago I was visiting Riverside, California, for a brief campaign (revival service) and was met at the train by the local Salvation Army captain (pastor) at about ten o'clock in the morning. His face was glowing as he said to me, "We got the worst old drunkard in town saved last night. And I have seen him twice this morning, and he is doing fine." How could the poor "old drunkard" do otherwise, with a captain bubbling over with faith, love, and good cheer, following him up like that? Don't forget, he saw the man twice the next morning. Twice! That is the way newborn babies are cared for, and that is the way to care for newborn souls.

This same captain came east to Pennsylvania and an evangelist visited his corps (church). That evangelist had about fifty people commit to following Christ, and the captain did not lose one but enrolled them all as soldiers (members). On another occasion, he labored until after midnight with a drunkard and then carried him to his lodging place on his back. The proprietor of the lodging house refused to receive him, but the captain carried the chap upstairs to his room, put him to bed, followed him up, and made a fully committed Salvation Army soldier out of him.

On the way home that night, long after midnight, the captain had to cross a great irrigation ditch, and when he came to the bridge he heard a splash and a groan. Rushing forward he found a man's feet sticking up, but his head under the bridge and under the water. He pulled the man out of the water and got the water out of him. The poor fellow—in a fit of discouragement—was trying to commit suicide. But the captain prayed with him, ushered him into the experience of salvation, and the man became an earnest Christian.

That Salvation Army officer is now a lieutenant colonel and a divisional commander and is still passionately seeking and looking after souls.

New followers of Jesus need care just as new babies do. Many years ago I was temporarily put in charge of the Chicago Number 1 Corps (church) for three weeks while awaiting the arrival of the newly appointed officer (minister) in charge. One night I met a man who was fifty years of age. He had been a builder and contractor but had met with reverses, and in his discouragement came to The Salvation Army and yielded to the Lord Jesus Christ. I took special interest in him and gave him a word of cheer and a hearty handshake in every meeting. But one night he failed to come, and I was anxious.

I could not call to see him that night, but I did write him a little note before going to bed and enclosed a little tract. I told him how greatly

I missed him, expressed my hope that he was well, urged him to look to Jesus if he were passing through any temptation, and told him I was praying for him and looked forward to seeing him the following evening. And, sure enough, he was present the next night, and he told me how he had been passing through a fierce temptation the day before and was just about to give up and go back to his old life when my letter with the little tract came with its message of love and faith.

"And that," said he, "saved me." He became a soldier and for years was a devoted Christian and worker for the Lord. The little note and tract and a two-cent stamp saved him.

If babies are to live, they must be nursed with tender care. If the flock is to be preserved, the lambs must be shepherded. If the world is to be saved, we must have new followers of Jesus, and they must be guarded with sleepless vigilance and followed with ceaseless and loving care.

# An Open Letter to a Young Man Seeking Spiritual Help

My Dear Comrade,

Your letter has just now reached me, and I hasten to reply.

You say, "I have sought and found holiness many times, but the longest I have been able to keep it was seven weeks." And then you mention some besetting sin against which you have struggled for five years.

Let me ask: Did you yield to this besetting sin? And then feeling condemned, did you come to the penitent form seeking a clean heart? If so, you have probably made the great mistake so many make of claiming heart purity when what you received was the peace of pardon. If I fall into sin, I must first confess my sin with a penitent heart and trust for pardon through reliance upon the blood of Jesus, and if I do this the peace of pardon will fill my heart. But I must not mistake this for sanctification.

When I am pardoned, I am then called to consecrate my redeemed life to God, and when I wholly consecrate myself to Him who has loved me out of my sins, guilt, and condemnation, I must trust Him to purify my whole being, to sanctify me wholly, and to fill me with the Holy Spirit. And if I believe, He can and will do the wonder work of grace in me. He will make me holy. He will perfect me in love. He will fill me with passion for His glory, so that I sing from my heart:

> Take my love, my Lord, I pour
> At Thy feet, its treasure store;
> Take my life and it shall be
> Ever, only, all for Thee.[1]

And with joy I sing:

> The blood, the blood is all my plea;
> Hallelujah! For it cleanses me.[2]

You speak of keeping the blessing seven weeks. How did you keep the blessing so long? Was it not by walking with the Blesser? If your attention is fixed upon the blessing instead of the Blesser—if you think of holiness as separate from the Holy Spirit—you will lose all. If you fail to recognize, honor, love, trust, and obey the Blesser, you lose the blessing, just as you lose the beauty of the rose when you turn your eyes from the rose, or the sweetness when you take away the honey, or the music when you lose the musician. Why and how did you lose the blessing after seven weeks? Was it not because under stress of temptation you took your eyes off the Blesser? You forgot the sweet, sacred presence of the Blesser and, turning from Him, you yielded to sin, or you doubted, and then the Enemy robbed you of the blessing.

"Watch and pray that you may not enter into temptation" (Matt. 26:41 ESV). When temptation came you should have said, "Get behind me, Satan" (Matt. 16:23 ESV). You should have resisted the Devil and drawn near to God (see James 4:7). The Blesser was there. The Holy Spirit was present. The infinitely loving Redeemer, with all His redemptive power, was with you, but you forgot Him, and so lost the blessing.

You should have turned to Jesus in love and loyalty and trust, and said, "O Lord, I am Yours; keep me! I trust You. I love You. I praise You, and I will not fear my Enemy." If you had done this, you would not have lost the blessing. "Resist the devil, and he will flee from you. Draw nigh to God, and he will draw nigh to you" (James 4:7–8 KJV). That is the way, and I know of no other way of victory. In that way, and that way only, I have been getting victory for nearly half a century, and in that way you can get victory, get it quickly, and get it always.

You are discouraged. You wonder if you can ever gain and keep the victory. You can! The victory is at the door now. The Victor is at the door. Open the door, let Him in, and victory is yours. Drop on your knees now, just now, and tell Him all. Then trust Him, thank Him, praise Him, whether or not you have any great feeling. Just keep on trusting, thanking, praising, and obeying Him, and peace and victory will come.

Keep your eyes on Jesus, and guard yourself against the beginnings of temptation and sin. Keep your mind pure. Fill it with clean thoughts, loving thoughts, and holy affections. Lift your thoughts above fleshly and low things to spiritual levels. Sing songs and make melody in your heart to the Lord.

Deal promptly and sternly with your eyes and your ears. Turn your eyes away from beholding evil and your ears from listening to evil. Make a covenant with your eyes as Job did (see Job 31:1). Stand on guard at eye-gate and ear-gate to see that sin does not get into your heart through those gateways.

Sin does not leap upon us fully armed. It steals in through a look, a swift and silent suggestion, or the imagination. But love and loyalty to Jesus will make you watchful and swift to rise up and cast out the subtle enemy. "Do this and you will live" (Luke 10:28 NLT) and live victoriously.

Often drop on your knees or lift your heart in secret prayer, and do not forget to mingle thanksgiving with your prayers. You do not praise God enough. Begin now. Thank Him now and praise Him, for He is worthy, and you are much behind in this sweet duty.

When you wake up in the morning ask Him for some verse of song to cheer you through the day, and find some verse of Scripture upon which to fix your mind. Finally, seek to pass some of your blessing on to some other soul, as the widow of Zarephath shared her bit of oil and handful of meal with Elijah and found it multiplying through the months of famine (see 1 Kings 17:7–16). So will you find your blessings multiplying as you share them with others.

### NOTES

1. Frances R. Havergal, "Take My Life and Let It Be," 1874, public domain.

2. E. F. Miller, "The Blood Is All My Plea," n. d., public domain.

# The Mystic Universe in My Backyard  18

I am not sure that I lived so intimately with my darling wife as I have for forty years lived with St. Paul. Far more constantly and intimately than he lived and traveled with his friend Barnabas and his young lieutenants—Silas, Titus, Epaphroditus, and Timothy—he has lived, traveled, slept, and talked with me, only I did the sleeping. I never found him napping. At any hour of the day or night, he was waiting wide awake and ready for me.

A text in John's first epistle and another in his gospel proved to be the open door to my soul, leading into the Holy of Holies, into the experience of cleansing and the spiritual vision and inward revelation of Christ. But I think Paul has been my greatest teacher and mentor, and my most intimate spiritual guide. But one thing I have not found in him—a love of nature. Some of his biographers think he had no such love. He traveled by sea and land, among great mountain passes in Cilicia, through the mountains of Macedonia, over the Balkan hills, over the blue Mediterranean, and among the lovely isles of Greece. But never once does he in any of his epistles mention the wonders of nature, the splendor of sky or sea, the glory and majesty of mountains, the beauty of flowers, or the flight of birds, except in his discussion of the resurrection of the body that springs from the sown seed and the difference in the glory of one star from another.

"There is one glory of the sun, another glory of the moon, and another glory of the stars; for one star differs from another star in glory" (1 Cor. 15:41 NKJV). The fact that there is such glory he admits, but there is nothing to indicate that he was ravished by that glory. Still, we have no right to say that he was not. He was writing epistles to the churches upon infinitely important ethical and spiritual subjects, and there was no occasion for him to enter into rapturous description and comments upon the wonders and beauty of nature. But in my forty years of intimate communion with him I have never once been inspired by him to look for the blinding glories of the passing days and seasons or the pop and splendor of starlit nights.

But not so when I turn to Job, to the psalms of David, to the proverbs and songs of Solomon, and to the sweet talks and parables of Jesus. There we see the sparrows feeding from the heavenly Father's hand, the ravens and the young lions and every creeping thing looking to Him for daily food, the fox fleeing from enemies to its hole, the conies among the rocks, the wild goat among mountain crags, the nesting bird, the busy ant, the swarming bees, the neighing warhorse, the spouting whale, the bridal lilies, the rose of Sharon, the green and smiling meadows, the still waters, the ice, the snow, the hoar frost, the glowing fire, the tempestuous wind and billowing seas, the lowering sky of the morning threatening rain and storm, and the red sky of the evening presaging fair and smiling weather. "The heavens proclaim the glory of God. The skies display his craftsmanship. Day after day they continue to speak; night after night they make him known" (Ps. 19:1–2 NLT). The vast deeps of the heavens are the tabernacle of the sun, which "bursts forth like a radiant bridegroom after his wedding [and] rejoices like a great athlete eager to run the race" (Ps. 19:5 NLT), the race course compasses the whole circle of heaven, and the whole creation in one vast antiphonal choral harmony praises God. So David sang.

But the suggestions, and beauty, and wonder, and mysticism in nature to which Paul has never turned me, but to which Jesus and Job and David and Solomon pointed me, I am now finding in large measure in my tiny backyard. I am discovering a universe in my backyard.

Early one January in the deep, dark, underground, crowded railway of New York, roaring along beneath the great city and plunging beneath the broad and lordly Hudson River, late at night after attending meetings and lecturing cadets, I became chilled. I awoke in the middle of the night to find my head and throat inflamed with a heavy cold. I spent two and a half days in bed under the doctor's care and then crawled out and went to Chicago, where a whirlwind campaign awaited me. I gave myself without stint to those meetings. Once, for the first time I could remember, I feared my chest would fail me as I gasped for breath while speaking. But oh, those meetings! They were times of heaven upon earth. At the last session, which continued from 3 to 7 p.m., the whole place seemed lit up by the reflected glory on the faces in the crowd.

At last, weary and happy, I boarded a train late at night for Texas. The temperature outside was zero, the snow was knee deep, and there was no heat in our car. I sat and shivered in my sweater, winter overcoat, and a big cape, and finally went to bed with my clothes on, still to shiver. When we got to Texas, I was aching in all my bones. For three weeks I fought on, and then the flu claimed me. For the next three weeks I was in bed, and for the next few weeks among pine woods trying to get back my strength.

Presently I came home, but could not walk the length of a city block without panting and gasping for a long breath. My doctor examined me, and then sat down silent and stern, looked at me, and then lectured me: "You have gone to the edge of the abyss. Stop now or you will stop with a crash from which you will find it hard, if not impossible, to recover. If you take my advice, you will stop for six months." He had warned me at other times, but I had not always listened to him—had laughed at him, in fact, and gone my own way. But somehow I felt he was right this time, and I would fail to heed him at a dread risk.

A further exhaustive physical examination revealed an impoverished state of my blood, not pernicious, but sufficiently grave for the doctors to say that I must keep in the sunshine and open air, live largely on green vegetables, and rest.

For nearly thirty years, by day and night, summer and winter, through long hours I had labored for souls and sung and prayed and preached in crowded, steaming, ill-ventilated auditoriums, pleading with listeners and dealing with penitents in an atmosphere so depleted of oxygen and poisoned that every pore of my body, every lung cell and red blood corpuscle cried out for fresh air. And now I have turned to my backyard to get what I need. It has been waiting for me for ten years. I saw no beauty in it that I desired it. But it holds no grudge, welcomes me now, and never hints at my lack of appreciation and my past neglect.

A clump of yellow and blue iris is in one corner. A flowering shrub that has never bloomed for eight years and may be cast out as an unprofitable cumberer of the ground is at one side. A rambler rose bush, now preparing to burst into a blaze of pink flame, and a crabapple tree (which I believe botanists say is a relative of the rose) occupy the center of the yard, and a few square yards of green grass sprawl around iris and shrub and tree.

Just outside the border of my backyard on one side is a big oak tree, and on another side a maple tree, and they cast cool shadows over the grass when the sun is hottest. Some distance away are a few other oak trees. One belongs to a robin and some English sparrows. Another belongs to two young grey squirrels who have bound themselves together by matrimonial ties and only yesterday built a nest for their prospective family in the fork of their tree out of leaves and twigs which they cut with their sharp teeth from tips of the far-reaching branches.

Yesterday one of them slyly visited the tree that belongs to the robin and sparrows. He watched cautiously and climbed quickly. There were some nests up there he hoped to find defenseless. But a sparrow's keen eyes spied him, and she sent out a far-reaching SOS. And from every quarter sparrows came, and then a robin. The *entente* was perfect. And then I heard fierce, shrill war cries and witnessed an aerial battle as thrilling after its kind as any fought over the forts and forests and fields of France. I laughed at the mischievous cunning and daring of the little robber, but I confess my sympathies were all with the allied forces. They chattered and screamed and dashed upon him with sharp beaks and rending little claws. They came from above and all sides, swift and sure, until he turned ignominiously and fled to escape with whole ears and unimpaired eyes. The little grey rascal! It was wilderness epic.

The trees are glorious. They are not so large as their forefathers, but I think of them as the heirs of all the ages. And as I look at their broad-reaching limbs and into their deep-green foliage, they suggest the dark, solemn, whispering, primeval forest that once clothed this continent with its sheen like a great green ocean. Right here the Native Americans, the bear, the deer, the skulking panther roamed only twice as long ago as the lifetime of those now living.

Swift, speeding automobiles and loud, rumbling trucks rush past my backyard, and I hear thundering trains and factory whistles not far away, but here in this wee enclosure, partly in fact and partly in imagination, I am living a wilderness life. An ocean of fresh air, fifty miles deep, washes me in its waves that beat upon all the shores and isles of seas, and the mountains and plains of all continents. And beams of sunshine ninety million miles long unerringly find me with their life-giving rays.

I would like to tell you about the ants and the big, fierce horseflies and the little flowers among the grass, so tiny and so shy as scarcely to be seen, which I have discovered in my backyard. The grass, to the little creatures who live among its spires and tangled masses, is a forest as vast and mysterious as the great forests that have disappeared before the ruthless onslaughts and march of humanity. They live and hunt their prey, and make love, and bring forth their young, and flee their enemies, and live their short little lives among the green aisles and shadows of the grass, and know nothing of the greater world that arches above them, with its strifes and loves and labor and aspiration and sin and shame and redemption.

The astronomers tells us that, so far as they can judge, there are many sidereal universes. The heaven of heavens is full of them. But if that is so, if there are many universes of the infinitely great in the vast abysses of space, then I am sure there are many universes of the infinitely little in my backyard, as dear to God as those composed of flaming stars. And if health and strength can be found in the wilderness of plain or forest, or on mountain or sea, I believe it can be found among the teeming wonders, the mystic universes, and in the ocean of air and sunshine I find in my backyard.

O Lord, I worship amid the wonders of Your creation and give You thanks for a contented mind and the wealthy heritage of my little backyard. Amen.

# The Frankness of Jesus 19

Jesus was not a whisperer. No one ever saw Him close to His neighbor's ear, looking stealthily around in case someone should overhear what He was going to say. He stood upright, looked others squarely and kindly in the eye, and spoke what He had to say right out, boldly, frankly, that the whole world might hear. And when He did speak privately to His disciples, He told them to shout it from the housetops. "Truth fears nothing but concealment," says an old proverb, and Jesus spoke only the truth: "To this end was I born, and for this cause came I into the world, that I should bear witness unto the truth" (John 18:37 KJV). He said, "What I tell you in the dark, say in the light, and what you hear whispered, proclaim on the housetops" (Matt. 10:27 ESV). It was against the Mosaic law to spread dangerous doctrines secretly, and the punishment was death (see Deut. 13:6–10). The High Priest and other religious leaders of Jesus' day had a right to inquire into this issue—indeed it was their duty to do so, according to their law, though they had no right to make Jesus convict Himself. However, that was not possible, for He had boldly preached His doctrine before priests and scribes as well as His disciples and the common people, and He answered the high priest: "Everyone knows what I teach. I have preached regularly in the synagogues and the Temple, where the people gather. I have not spoken in secret" (John 18:20 NLT). This refers to Jesus' doctrine, but can it not be given a far wider meaning? Was not His whole life an open book? Was not all His conversation such as could be proclaimed openly to the whole world?

There was nothing dark and hidden about Jesus. He was and is the Light of the World, and He welcomed the light. He entered into no secret cabals and councils. He belonged to no clique or party faction. I really do not believe He would have joined a secret society for two reasons. First, because if there was anything wrong and dark about it, His pure spirit, His guileless soul, would have revolted and denounced and withdrawn from it. And second, because if there was anything good in it, His generous spirit, His loving soul, overflowing with pity and goodwill, would never have been content till the whole world knew about it and had the privilege of sharing in its benefits. A good thing that He could not offer to share with all would have ceased to be a good thing to Jesus.

An astute Frenchman once said to The Salvation Army's founder, "General Booth, you are not an Englishman, you're a citizen of the world. You belong to humanity." And in this the general was like his Master. Jesus belonged to the world. He was the Son of Man, the Son of humanity. No party could claim Him. Thomas Jefferson wrote, "If I could not go to heaven but with a party, I would not go there at all."[1]

It was this generous, open, worldwide, selfless spirit of Jesus that made Him so frank in all His speech, so that at the end of His life and His brief but complicated ministry, in which His enemies had sought in every way to provoke and entrap Him, He could say, "I have not spoken in secret" (John 18:20 NLT).

And now He wants us to "follow his steps: Who did no sin, neither was guile found in his mouth: Who, when he was reviled, reviled not again; when he suffered, he threatened not" (1 Pet. 2:21–23 KJV). If we do this we shall not be talebearers, we shall not listen to nor pass on gossip, nor be whisperers. "A whisperer separates close friends," said Solomon (Prov. 16:28 ESV). He also said, "Where there is no whisperer, quarreling ceases" (Prov. 26:20 ESV). And Paul linked "whisperers"— people who go around saying things in secret that they are afraid to say out boldly to everybody—with fornicators, murderers, backbiters, and haters of God (see Rom. 1:29–30). And one of the accursed things he feared for his beloved church in Corinth was "whisperings" (2 Cor. 12:20 KJV).

People who speak in secret what they are afraid to speak openly wrong their own souls, weaken their own character, and corrupt themselves, and those who listen to them are filled with suspicions and dislikes, destroying the beautiful spirit of brotherly love, which is open-faced, frank, generous, and saving in its power. Such whisperings quench the spirit of prayer and cause faith in God and others to languish and possibly die—for faith can live and flourish only in an atmosphere of frankness, kindness, and goodwill.

## NOTE

1. Thomas Jefferson, *The Writings of Thomas Jefferson*, vol. 2 (Boston: Gray and Bowen, 1830), 439.

# Our Mothers

How fitting, how beautiful, that a day should be set aside by the nation and the nations to honor that vast army of delicate soldiers, infinitely greater in numbers than the men who fought in the Great War, that numberless host whose sentinel watch is never done, whose arms are never laid down, whose warfare permits no discharge, and in which there is never an armistice until they fall on the field of battle: the great army of mothers.

We hail them and do them honor. They are a sacrificial host, the great givers and sufferers of the race. We never see a strong man striding forth in his strength for whom some mother has not suffered and given of her strength. We never see a blooming girl with rosy cheeks and laughing eyes and bewitching curls for whom some mother has not given of her own bloom and beauty and youth.

They bleed that we may be blessed. They keep watch that we may take rest and sleep. They suffer and often die that we may live.

Our mothers are our comforters in sorrow and the healers of our hearts when they are hurt. When the little child cries with loneliness in the dark and still night, and sobs and moans and reaches out little hands and arms, it is for Mother. When the child is hurt, he or she runs to Mother and finds balm in her kiss and comfort in the warmth and tenderness of her encircling arms for all fear and grief and healing for every wound.

When the big, foolish, awkward boy has a problem that perplexes, a hunger to satisfy, a shame to confess, or a triumph to announce, he goes to Mother, for she will understand. When the strong man is wearied by the toil and strife of life and his heart is harassed by uncertainties and doubt, he turns to Mother and Mother's God.

And when at last death wrestles with men and women, tightens its icy fingers upon them, and mocks them and claims them for its own as their strength fails, how often their thoughts turn to Mother! When stern old Thomas Carlyle lay dying, he was asked if there was anything he wanted. Turning his face to the wall, the granite of his Scotch heart broke up, and the old man sobbed, "I want ma mither." In the hour of death his heart turned as a little child to his mother.

Here is the might and the responsibility of motherhood. She can hold her children to goodness and God, not by force but by affection, not by the compulsion of command but by the compulsion of high and holy character.

I have been asked how mothers can hold their boys and keep them in paths of rectitude and godliness, and I can only reply to such questioning mothers, "You will help your boys not so much by what you say as by what you are and what you do. Command their respect, their admiration, and their love by loftiness and firmness of character, by patient steadfastness in well doing, by sweetness of spirit, by gentleness and graciousness of speech, and by the power of the Spirit of Christ abiding ungrieved in your cleansed heart, and though they may for a time wander away from you, yet unseen chains still bind them to you, and they will return, drawn back by mysterious cords of love and reverence."

Abraham Lincoln's mother died when he was only eight years old, but at the height of his fame and power he said, "All I am I owe to my angel mother."

I had just passed my fifteenth birthday and was away at school when one day the first telegram I ever received was handed to me. I read, "Come home, come quickly, mother is dying!" When I got home, she was dead. For the next twelve years, I had no home. I went off to school and college, but I received no letters from home. When holiday time came, I saw the other students trooping to the train with laughter, for they were going home, but I stayed behind, for no home awaited me. But my mother's sweet face was ever before me. Her love-lit eyes were ever turned upon me, so it seemed to me, and if ever I was tempted to evil, grief and reproach seemed to fill her eyes, while I could see love and sweet joy beaming in her face and from her eyes when I resisted the temptation. Indeed, her memory and influence were like a presence ever before and around me, and were like a flaming shield between me and youth's temptations. And I have known many a boy whose love and high and tender regard and reverence for his mother were like a pillar of fire and cloud to guide and protect him by day and by night. One boy I know intimately wrote to his mother and told her she was to him as "a piece of God, a dear little piece of God." And every mother should be to her boys and girls as "a piece of God, a dear little piece of God." And so she may be if she loves God with all her heart and seeks in all her words and ways to represent Him to her children.

Some mothers are not worthy of the love and respect of their children. A little orphaned boy was committed to one of our children's homes, and in its sweet and sacred atmosphere he was convicted of sin, but he said, "I can't get saved. When my mother was dying, I spit in her face." Her wickedness had reproduced itself in her little boy, and strangers had to undo the deadly work wrought in his poor little child heart by her sin.

It is religion pure and undefiled that crowns motherhood.

The glory of motherhood is the glory of sacrifice. A little lad noticed that tradesmen presented his mother with a bill for service. So a happy thought wakened within him and he presented a bill:

Mother debtor to Tommy:

| | |
|---|---|
| Minding the baby | $6 |
| Chopping and bringing in wood | $9 |
| Mailing letters for a week | $10 |
| Going to the shop | $6 |
| TOTAL | $29 |

He laid it on her plate at the table. Mother looked at it, smiled, and then grew serious. At the next meal, Tommy found a bill at his plate:

Tommy debtor to Mother:

| | |
|---|---|
| For caring for him through years of infancy | $0 |
| For nursing him through two dangerous illnesses | $0 |
| For getting his meals for him for ten years every day | $0 |
| For washing and mending his clothes | $0 |
| TOTAL | $0 |

Poor Tommy! When he read it, the long sacrifice and unwearied devotion of his mother dawned upon him, and with tears in his eyes he threw his arms around his mother and begged pardon for his thoughtlessness.

The glory of motherhood is the glory of unfailing patience. The father of John and Charles Wesley said to Susanna, their mother, one day, "Mother, why do you tell Charles the same thing over twenty times?"

She quietly replied, "Because nineteen times won't do."

Oh, the patience of mothers!

The glory of motherhood is the glory of unwavering faith and undying hope. A mother dedicated her baby to God and in prayer felt a conviction and assurance that he would preach the gospel. But instead of giving his heart to God, he fell into sin, and instead of preaching, he became a drunken unbeliever, mouthing infidelity. But the mother still prayed and believed and hoped on. One day she was sent for and told that he was dying of delirium tremens. She went quietly to his home, saying, "He is not dying. He will live and yet preach the gospel." And he did live. And he did preach the gospel—like a living flame of fire. And years later his sweet granddaughter also preached the gospel in The Salvation Army.

The glory of motherhood is the glory of self-forgetful unselfishness. A Salvation Army mother with six sons and daughters in the Army's work lay dying. Her youngest daughter, a cadet (student) in training for ministry, hastened to her side. But the saintly mother said, "Dear, I shall be cared for. I dedicated you, and God has called you to His work. Return to the training school and continue your studies. We shall meet in the morning at home in heaven." The dying mother forgot herself in her love for Christ and her holy ambition for her child.

The glory of motherhood is the glory of love that never fails. Some time ago, I was in a city where a large state prison is located. In my meetings in that city I noticed a sweet-faced, tiny woman with silvery hair and the peace of God in her face. One Sunday we went to the prison for a service with the prisoners and she was there. Her boy—I think he was her only boy—had wandered from home, fallen in with evil people, and was shut in behind the grim prison walls. When the little mother heard the heartbreaking news, all the tender love of her heart for her wayward boy burst into flame, and she left her home in the north and came to this city to live, that she might be near her son. And every Sunday she went to the prison to see him, seeking to win him back to goodness and God.

You can never wear it out, mother love is strong;
It will live through sin and shame, hurt and cruel wrong;
Even though the world revile and your friendships die,
Though your hands be black with sin, she will hear your cry,
Still she'll love you and forgive.[1]

Such is the glory of all true mothers, and for them we give praise to God, and to them we give the tribute of our reverence and tenderest affection.

> The bravest battles that were ever fought,
> Shall I tell you where and when?
> On the map of the world you'll find it not,
> 'Twas fought by the mothers of men.
>
> Nay, not with cannon or battle shot,
> With sword or noble pen.
> Nay, not with eloquent word or thought
> From mouths of wonderful men;
>
> But deep in a walled-up woman's heart—
> A woman that would not yield,
> But bravely, silently bore her part;
> Lo, there is that battlefield.
>
> No marshalling of troops, no bivouac song,
> No banners to gleam and wave;
> But oh! these battles they last so long,
> From babyhood to the grave.[2]

### NOTES

1. Edgar A. Guest, "Mother," 1925, public domain.
2. Joaquin Miller, "Mothers of Men," 1924, public domain.

# Jesus Training Paul  21

We learn from the Gospels how Jesus, in the days of His flesh, trained the Twelve. We learn from the Acts and Paul's letters how the risen and glorified Jesus trained Paul. This chapter is a fragmentary study of that training and of some of Paul's struggles, inner conflicts, and fears out of and through which he was trained to triumph by obedient faith.

His experience was not one of ceaseless calm. Storms swept over him. It was not one of perpetual open vision. He was compelled to walk by faith and not by sight. He was sent forth to be a pathfinder, and no pathfinder treads an easy way, whether it is across trackless wastes of sand and sea; through the tangled jungles of a tropical forest; or amid the denser, darker jungles of base, idolatrous superstitions and bloody and licentious rites, or the claims of a cold, self-satisfied, arrogant, petrified priesthood.

Paul was treading a way that no one had trod before him. He had turned his back on all his teachers and all the traditions of his people and was carrying the gospel to the Gentiles, and what he spoke and wrote he learned from no man or woman. A strange, glorious, divine experience had come to him on the road to Damascus and in the street called Straight. But it had to be interpreted, and he found no interpreter. For three years, in the solitude of Arabia and in the silences of the night, he wrestled with his problems and the Lord illumined him, and he began to see new meanings in the ancient Scriptures. They ceased to be a binding, deadening letter and became life and spirit. His mind was liberated as from chains. God ceased to be simply the God of the Jews, a national God. He was the heavenly Father to whom all are dear, and the Lord Jesus Christ was not simply a Messiah for one people, a military conqueror, winning and building up His kingdom by the power of His sword. He was "the desire of all nations" (Hag. 2:7 KJV), bringing spiritual deliverance to all, not with sword and battle and "garments rolled in blood" (Isa. 9:5 KJV), but by the shame and power of the cross, winning His kingdom not by the slaughter of His enemies, but by becoming the Suffering Servant of all.

In Paul's letters, and especially in his letter to the Romans, we find many quotations from the Psalms and the old prophets, and these quotations are portions of the ancient Scriptures into which the Holy Spirit was flashing new meanings to Paul's mind. They became the sheet anchor of his faith when storms swept over his soul and bitter enemies denounced his claims to be an apostle.

One day his call came. The risen Jesus spoke to him and appointed him to be the apostle to the Gentiles. He wanted to stay at home and preach to his own people, but the Lord said, "They will not accept your testimony about me." But Paul argued back, "Lord, they themselves know that in one synagogue after another I imprisoned and beat those who believed in you. And when the blood of Stephen your witness was being shed, I myself was standing by and approving and watching over the garments of those who killed him." Surely, thought Paul, they will—they must—receive my testimony. Little did he yet know the willful stubbornness and fierce bigotry of unbelief. But the call was insistent: "Go, for I will send you far away to the Gentiles" (Acts 22:18–21 ESV). And Paul "was not disobedient to the heavenly vision" (Acts 26:19 ESV).

"I will show him how much he must suffer for the sake of my name," said Jesus to Ananias, when He sent him to the blinded Saul that he might receive his sight and be filled with the Holy Spirit (Acts 9:16 ESV). Little did Paul know what lay before him in the untrodden future. That was graciously hidden from him as it is from you and me.

There is a threefold ministry to which we are called: the ministry of service, the ministry of sacrifice, and the ministry of suffering. Some people seem called and fitted for one and some for another, but Paul was called and chosen to each and all of these ways of ministering the gospel. Great things he suffered. Great sacrifices were demanded of him. Immeasurable toil and great and insistent cares pressed ceaselessly upon him. Body, mind, and soul were each taxed to the limit in his great task. It was not always by some open vision or cheering voice, but often by the things he suffered that his Master taught and fashioned him.

Once in Asia some great trouble befell him, and he wrote, "We were burdened beyond measure, above strength, so that we despaired even of life. Yes, we had the sentence of death in ourselves, that we should not trust in ourselves but in God who raises the dead, who delivered us from so great a death" (2 Cor. 1:8–10 NKJV). In such manner Jesus trained and developed the faith of Paul and taught him to trust only in God. Could He not have taught Paul to trust in some easier way? Possibly, but He chose that way, and it must have been the best way. Paul was strong and self-reliant, and like Jacob at Jabbok, whose thigh was disjointed, he had to be broken to become "as a prince" and have "power with God and with men" (Gen. 32:28 KJV).

In his letter to the Thessalonian church, he exhorted them to "comfort the feebleminded, support the weak, be patient toward all" (1 Thess. 5:14 KJV). How did Paul, with his trained and master mind, learn to be gentle with the feebleminded, "as a nursing mother cherishes her own children" (1 Thess. 2:7 NKJV)? How, with his passionate, aggressive nature, did he come to put his strength at the disposal of the weak? How, with his impetuous and fiery spirit, did he ever become "patient toward all"? Like his Master, who, in the days of His humanity, "learned . . . obedience by the things which he suffered" (Heb. 5:8 KJV), so Paul was trained and so he learned from Jesus in the school of suffering.

We see how latent lightnings in his soul could flash and leap forth like a thunderbolt in his retort to the high priest who had commanded him to be smitten on the mouth: "God will slap you, you corrupt hypocrite! What kind of judge are you to break the law yourself by ordering me struck like that?" (Acts 23:3 NLT). It is true that when rebuked for so speaking to the high priest, he meekly replied, "'I'm sorry, brothers. I didn't realize he was the high priest . . . for the Scriptures say, 'You must not speak evil of any of your rulers'" (Acts 23:5 NLT).

But would Jesus have retorted as Paul did? When He was smitten by an officer because of His perfectly reasonable answer to the high priest, Jesus quietly said, "If I said anything wrong, you must prove it. But if I'm speaking the truth, why are you beating me?" (John 18:23 NLT).

Who am I that I should presume to judge Paul? I dare not judge him. I love him too tenderly. I have lived with him too intimately for over forty years. I am too greatly awed by his sacrificial life, his lofty character, his Christlike spirit, to attempt to pass judgment upon him. But if in that retort he fell below the standard of the Master, how is his spirit to be made meek and lowly as the Master?

"I, Paul, myself entreat you, by the meekness and gentleness of Christ," he wrote the Corinthians (2 Cor. 10:1 ESV). How did he learn this meekness and gentleness of Christ? There is but one way. "Take my yoke upon you, and learn of me," said Jesus, "for I am meek and lowly in heart" (Matt. 11:29 KJV). Paul came to Jesus, took upon himself the yoke of Jesus, received the spirit of Jesus, and submitted wholeheartedly without murmuring and complaint or self-pity to the discipline of Jesus, and so learned his lessons. From the day Jesus met him on the Damascus road, he was no longer persecuting" (see Acts 9:5). He might stand up stoutly against a traducer, but he bowed instantly at the word of Jesus. "The sinful nature [which] is always hostile to God" (Rom. 8:7 NLT) went out of him forever, and he followed Jesus with the passionate ardor of the perfect lover and the docility of the slave of love. Inbred sin is that something within that leads us to selfishly seek our own way instead of God's way, our own pleasure instead of God's pleasure—that exalts itself, that frets and repines or stubbornly resists in the presence of God's will. From all this Paul was set free.

That was the law—the power—of sin and death (see Rom. 8:2), and with that he had painfully and hopelessly struggled until he felt that he was like the ancient Etrurian murderer—who for punishment was chained face-to-face, chin-to-chin, limb-to-limb, to his dead, rotting, putrefying victim—and he cried out, "O wretched man that I am, who shall deliver me from this dead body?" (Rom. 7:24, paraphrase). But upon meeting Jesus, believing in Jesus, casting himself in self-despair upon Jesus, and yielding to Jesus, Paul exultingly cried out, "There is therefore now no condemnation to those who are in Christ Jesus, who do not walk according to the flesh, but according to the Spirit. For the law of the Spirit of life in Christ Jesus has made me free from the law of sin and death" (Rom. 8:1–2 NKJV). His heart was pure of sin, but purity is not maturity. Purity comes instantly when the surrendered, pardoned soul intelligently and gladly, in simple faith, yields all its redeemed faculties and powers in an utter, unconditional, irreversible dedication to its Lord. But the ripe mellowness, the serene wisdom, the Christlike composure of maturity can only come through manifold experiences as we walk with Jesus in service, sacrifice, and suffering, and learn from Him.

Paul's spirit had to be disciplined, and he had much to learn as well as much to suffer. When Jesus commissioned him, He said, "I have appeared to you for this purpose, to appoint you as a servant and witness to the things in which you have seen me"—the things he had already learned—"and to those in which I will appear to you" (Acts 26:16 ESV). So the teaching and training and maturing of Paul began and continued through the years until at last he could write, "The time of my departure is at hand. I have fought a good fight, I have finished my course, I have kept the faith" (2 Tim. 4:6–7 KJV).

His Lord did not spare him, but He never failed him. And so out of wide experience and intimate knowledge Paul could write letters that were the revelation of the plan, the purpose, the mind, and the character of God in Christ—letters that have come down across two thousand years and are still as sweet and fresh and life-giving as clear waters from everlasting springs, bubbling up in deep, cool valleys, fed by eternal snows from great mountains.

Jesus meant, and Paul felt, that his experiences were not for himself alone. Through him Jesus was teaching the whole church for all time—teaching you and me. When in Paul's sore trials and tribulations his faithful Lord comforted him, he said that it was that he might comfort others with the comfort he had received from God, "For just as we share abundantly in the sufferings of Christ, so also our comfort abounds through Christ. If we are distressed, it is for your comfort and salvation; if we are comforted, it is for your comfort" (2 Cor. 1:5–6 NIV).

We may be sure that when Paul wrote, he wrote out of experience. When he wrote to those he loved at Ephesus, "Put on the full armor of God, so that you can take your stand against the devil's schemes" (Eph. 6:11 NIV), we rest assured that he had firsthand knowledge of those wiles and of the hopelessness of any defense unless we are arrayed in the whole armor of God. When he wrote, "In addition to all this, take up the shield of faith, with which you can extinguish all the flaming arrows of the evil one" (Eph. 6:16 NIV), there surely flashed into his memory some dark and lonely, painful and prolonged period when the Archenemy of his soul plied him with questionings and doubts and fears and forebodings for the future, and accusations for the past, until his harassed soul seemed to him like some soldier on the battlefield who was the target of archers who had dipped their darts in pitch and flame, and against which darts his only defense was his shield, the shield of faith. Those darts would quench their flame in his lifeblood if he did not use this shield, but against it they fell harmless.

In his first letter to the Thessalonians, he reminded them that in spite of the painful and shameful and dangerous treatment he received at Philippi, "We were bold in our God to speak unto you the gospel of God with much contention" (1 Thess. 2:2 KJV). Bold. But listen. In his letter to the Ephesians, written from Rome—where, he said, he was "an ambassador in chains"—he asked for church's prayers that "I may speak boldly, as I ought to speak" (Eph. 6:20 NKJV). Do we not get a hint from this of the temptation from which he suffered, and against which he girded himself and asked the sympathetic help of his brothers and sisters? He was old and worn, bruised and scarred, chained in prison and surrounded by relentless foes, and he was tempted to timidity and cowardice in preaching his gospel. Dear old Paul. Like his Master and ours, he was "tempted in every way, just as we are" (Heb. 4:15 NIV). But he fought on and triumphed. It is no sin to be tempted. It is sinful to yield. Paul did not yield, and so he remained in the school of Christ, and so Christ trained him.

It was out of such manifold experiences that he could write with an assurance that has reassured myriads of tempted, harassed souls, "No temptation has overtaken you that is not common to man. God is faithful, and he will not let you be tempted beyond your ability, but with the temptation he will also provide the way of escape, that you may be able to endure it" (1 Cor. 10:13 ESV).

Paul had mountain peak and paradisiacal experiences, but he also had hours of depression. How could it be otherwise, unless miracles had periodically been wrought for his deliverance?

Jesus would not turn stones into bread to satisfy His own hunger after forty days of fasting. And in training Paul, He did not pet and pamper and so spoil him. Heroes, martyrs, world conquerors, saints, are not made that way. "What are these which are arrayed in white robes? And whence came they?" asked John in Revelation. "These are they which came out of great tribulation, and have washed their robes, and made them white in the blood of the Lamb," was the answer (Rev. 7:13–14 KJV). Paul had great tribulation, and how could he escape the depression of reaction, when bruised from beatings and stonings, smarting and bleeding from cruel whippings, hungry and thirsty, pinched with cold, and exhausted from shipwreck and long and painful journeys? Add to these physical hardships his constant "care of all the churches" (2 Cor. 11:28 KJV), and his anxiety for his poor, persecuted churches in far-off cities. Add further his constant danger from relentless enemies who followed him from city to city. And, finally, add to all these Satan's hellish darts, and we get some conception of the infirmities, reproaches, necessities, persecutions, and distresses in and through which Jesus trained, disciplined, beautified, enriched, perfected, and matured the spirit of Paul, until he gloried and took pleasure in his infirmities, for in these it was revealed to his faith, rather than in his own native strength and powers, the power of Christ rested upon him. He said, "I have learned"—and learning is a process often prolonged and painful—"in whatsoever state I am, therewith to be content. I know both how to be abased, and I know how to abound"—a very difficult lesson, and one very dangerous not to learn. "Every where and in all things I am instructed"—still in the school of Christ—"both to be full and to be hungry, both to abound and to suffer need. I can do all things through Christ which [strengthens] me" (Phil. 4:11–13 KJV).

I see Your school is not an easy one, O Christ, but I would learn from You. Train me; teach me. Do You reply to me as to James and John, "You do not know not what you ask"? Still, O Lord, train me, discipline me, teach me. Do You ask, "Are you able to drink the cup that I am about to drink, and be baptized with the baptism that I am baptized with" (Matt. 20:22 NKJV)? You know, O Lord. I trust Your love and Your wisdom, and into Your hands I commit my spirit. So, teach me and train me that I with Paul may know You and the power of Your resurrection and the fellowship of Your sufferings, that I may comprehend with all the saints what is the breadth, and length, and depth, and height, and know the love of Christ, which surpasses knowledge, that I may be filled with all the fullness of God and thereby show to this generation Your strength, and Your power to everyone that is to come.

# *A Second Wind*  22

When I was a little lad, time went by so slowly and the years seemed so long that I felt I would never be a man. But I was told that the years would not seem so long when I got into my teens. So I waited in hope, and after what seemed a century or two, I reached my teens, and sure enough the years tripped by a bit more quickly. Then I got into my twenties and they sped by yet more swiftly, and I reached my thirties and speedily passed into my forties. And almost before I had time to turn around I found myself in my fifties. About the time I hoped to catch my breath, the wild rush of years carried me into my sixties, and now I'm bracing myself for the plunge into the abyss of retirement!

But is it an abyss? Will it swallow me up, and shall I be lost in its dark and silent depths? Is it not rather a sun-kissed, peaceful slope on the sunset side of life where my often over-tasked body can have a measure of repose, and my spirit, freed in part from the driving claims of spiritual warfare, can have a foretaste of the Sabbath calm of eternity?

Well, I shall soon know, for—abyss or sunlit slope—it is just ahead of me. In a very little while I shall find my name in the list of those who are retired. However, I am not distressed in the least about this, but I am thinking about it and laying spiritual anchors to windward against that day.

I know that Jesus said, "Take therefore no thought for the morrow, for the morrow shall take thought for the things of itself" (Matt. 6:34 KJV). But I am sure He did not mean that literally, for if so, we should never buy supplies or set aside money for taxes or a new suit of clothes. What He meant was that we should take no anxious thought. We should not worry and fret about tomorrow.

The best way I know to avoid anxious thought is to take calm, prayerful forethought. So I am taking forethought against the day of my retirement. I am praying for grace and wisdom for that time, and already I am considering what seem to me to be possible dangers and arming my spirit in advance against them. I believe in preparedness. Jesus said, "Be ready all the time" (Matt. 24:44 NLT). So I watch and pray and prepare, that I may not be found wanting. I don't want to lose the dew from my soul. The dew of the morning passes away but there is also the dew of evening—I do not want to miss that.

Sunset is often as glorious as sunrise, and when the sun goes down "the eternal stars shine out."[1] Often the splendor of the night is more wonderful than that of the day. The sun reveals the little things—the flowers and grasses and birds and hills and sea and mountains. But the larger things—the immensities of the heavens with their flashing meteors, their silvery moons, their star-strewn depths sown thick with flaming suns—these are the great things, and they are hidden by the garish light of day but revealed by the kindly darkness of night.

So I suspect the greater glories, the surpassing splendors of the spiritual world, are yet to be revealed to me as the sun of this life begins to sink beneath western hills. "At evening time it shall be light" (Zech. 14:7 KJV). I do not expect to fold my hands and sit in listless idleness or vain repining when I am retired. There will still be abundant work for my head and heart and hands. I shall probably not be so active on the field of ministry, or be going to and fro in the earth on long campaigns as in the past. But I hope to pray more for my comrades who are on the field and in the thick of the fight. There will be plenty of knee work to do, and we have need of knee workers more than ever, for this kaleidoscopic age—electric, restless, and changeful as the wind-swept sea—does not lend itself to prayer, the prayer that gets into close grips with God and the great wants of men and women, and brings down heavenly resources to meet vast earthly needs.

I shall meditate more—at least I hope to—and read and ponder my Bible more, and try to match its wondrous truths with life, the life I still live and must live. And by its light I shall try to interpret the life that surges all around me and manifests itself in the great movements, the triumphs and agonies and birth throes of peoples and nations. Oh, it will be a fascinating study!

I shall find plenty to do. If I can't command a Salvation Army corps or division, or take part in councils, or lead great soul-saving campaigns, I can talk to my grocer and doctor and letter-carrier about Jesus crucified and glorified, and the life that is everlasting. I can wear my (Salvation Army) uniform and go to testify. And I can still take an interest in the children and young people, and maybe out of the books of my experience find some helpful life lessons for them. And in doing this I shall hope to keep my own spirit young and resilient and sympathetic. I don't want to become hard and blind and unsympathetic toward youth, with its pathetic ignorance and conceit, its spiritual dangers, its heart-hunger, its gropings after experiences that satisfy, and its eager haste and its ardent ambitions.

I can write letters to struggling pastors—letters of congratulation for those who are winning victory; letters of sympathy and cheer for those who are being hard pressed by the foe; letters to missionaries in far-off lands; and letters to those who are bereaved, who sit with empty arms and broken hearts in the dark shadows and deep silence beside open graves where I too have sat, whose heartache and deep grief I know, who in vain long "for the touch of a vanished hand, and the sound of a voice that is still."[2]

I can write letters to those who in pain and weariness and possible loneliness are nearing the valley of the shadow of death, where only the Good Shepherd can go with them every step of the way, but where some word of hope and cheer may still reach them from someone who thinks of them in love and ceases not to pray for them.

The thought of retirement does not frighten me, nor cause me to repine, nor kindle resentment in me. Indeed, my long and somewhat heavy and exacting campaigns have left me frequently so weary that my body has cried out, "Here, now, you have driven me long enough; I am out of breath, exhausted, wearied half to death, tired down to the ground. I want you to retire."

But then my spirit has risen up and cried out, "Not a bit of it. Don't think of retirement! I'm not weary. I'm just learning how to fight. I'm getting my second wind. I want to die in the thick of the conflict on the field, at the battle's front, sword in hand, with my boots on."

So there is my problem. Retirement will give my body a breathing spell, but I am studying how to satisfy my spirit and give it worthy employment, with scope to fly and run and walk and not grow weary (see Isa. 40:31). Well, I shall find a way! Paul did, and Bunyan, and blessed and beloved old John on Patmos. Paul was sent to prison, but he talked to his guards and won them to Christ, and before long there were saints in Caesar's household (see Phil. 4:22). And, oh, those prison letters! Why, we would have missed some of the most precious portions of the Bible if Paul had not been forced into retirement through his prison experiences. I am glad he did not sit down and curse his fate and find fault and let his hands hang down and his knees grow feeble, but still strove on and made the years of retirement supplement and complete the labors of his active years.

John found work in his retirement. "Your old men shall dream dreams, your young men shall see visions," said Joel (Joel 2:28 KJV). But John, in his old age, banished to the Isle of Patmos, swept by wintry seas, reversed the order of Joel and saw visions. "I saw, I heard," wrote John. What did he see?

"I saw a great white throne, and him that sat on it" (Rev. 20:11 KJV). "I saw a new heaven and a new earth" (Rev. 21:1 KJV). "I . . . saw the holy city, new Jerusalem, coming down from God out of heaven" (Rev. 21:2 KJV). "I saw the dead, small and great, stand before God" (Rev. 20:12 KJV).

What did he hear?

I heard a loud shout from the throne, saying, "Look, God's home is now among his people! He will live with them, and they will be his people. God himself will be with them. He will wipe every tear from their eyes, and there will be no more death or sorrow or crying or pain. All these things are gone forever. . . .

"All who are victorious will inherit all these blessings, and I will be their God, and they will be my children. But cowards, unbelievers, the corrupt, murderers, the immoral, those who practice witchcraft, idol worshipers, and all liars—their fate is in the fiery lake of burning sulfur. This is the second death." (Rev. 21:3–4, 7–8 NLT)

One day I went through the book of Revelation and noted the things John saw, and the things John heard. And it occurred to me that God is no respecter of persons, but is eternally the same, and if John had visions and heard angelic voices in retirement, may not I? Bunyan the tinker did. In his filthy jail, surrounded by ignorance and vileness, in poverty and distress, oppressed by hard confinement, he caught visions of heaven and hell and delectable mountains and angelic hosts that made his retirement so fruitful as to feed the whole church of God for ages upon ages.

Even poor blind old Samson, sent into dark and bitter retirement through his sin, at last groped his way back to God, wrought havoc among the enemies of the Lord and of His people, and accomplished more in his death than in his life.

So when I am retired I shall not sulk in my tent, nor repine, nor grumble at my lot. Nor shall I seek a secular job to while away my time. For years I resisted God's call to preach. My heart was set on being a lawyer. But against my protest and stubborn resistance was God's insistent call. And since "the gifts and the calling of God are irrevocable" (Rom. 11:29 ESV), and since "God has given me this sacred trust" (1 Cor. 9:17 NLT), I shall carry on and do with my might what my hands find to do, and do so with joy and good cheer. But,

> My soul, be on thy guard,
> Ten thousand foes arise;
> The hosts of sin are pressing hard
> To draw thee from the skies.
>
> Ne'er think the battle won,
> Nor lay thine armor down;
> The fight of faith will not be done
> Till thou obtain the crown.[3]

Oh, my soul,

> Be sober, then, be vigilant; forbear
> To seek or covet aught beyond thy sphere;
> Only be strong to labor, and allow
> Thy Master's will to appoint thee where and how.
> Serve God! And winter's cold, or summer's heat,
> The breezy mountains or the dusty street—

Scene, season, circumstance, alike shall be

His welcome messengers of joy to thee,

His 'kingdom is within thee': rise, and prove

A present earnest of the bliss above![4]

And rejoice, oh my soul,

In the hour of death, after this life's whim,

When the heart beats low, and the eyes grow dim,

And pain has exhausted every limb—

The lover of the Lord shall trust in Him.

When the will has forgotten the lifelong aim,

And the mind can only disgrace its fame,

And man is uncertain of his own name—

The power of the Lord shall fill this frame.

When the last sigh is heard, and the last tear shed,

And the coffin is waiting beside the bed,

And the widow and child forsake the dead—

The angel of the Lord shall lift this head.

For even the purest delight may pall,

And power must fail and the pride must fall,

And the love of the dearest friends grow small—

But the glory of the Lord is all in all.[5]

## NOTES

1. Thomas Carlyle, as quoted in Charles Noel Douglas, comp., *Forty Thousand Quotations: Prose and Poetical* (New York: Halcyon House, 1917), 42.

2. Alfred Lord Tennyson, "Break, Break, Break," 1835, public domain.

3. George Heath, "My Soul, Be on Thy Guard," 1781, public domain.

4. T. E. Hankinson, "The Cross Planted upon the Himalaya Mountains," *Poems* (London: Hatchard and Company, 1860), 300–301.

5. Richard Doddridge Blackmore, "At the Last," n. d., public domain.

# The Future of
# The Salvation Army

There are some questions always being asked and never fully answered, for the simple reason that only omniscience knows the answer. And omniscience is not disposed to answer questions which can be solved in some measure by diligent attention to the Spirit and principles revealed in the Bible, and the final answer to which is largely contingent upon our good behavior, our humility, our loyalty to truth and love, our unswerving allegiance to Jesus, and our diligence in keeping His commandments and walking in His footsteps.

I have recently been asked what I think about the future of The Salvation Army.[1] This is an old question, about as old as the Army itself. It was making the rounds when I joined the Army over forty years ago, and someone has been asking it ever since. Both friends and foes of The Salvation Army have asked it. Officers (ministers) and soldiers (church members) lives and whose families have been linked up and entwined with the Army have asked it. And I doubt not that our leaders have pondered over it and given it their profoundest and most anxious thought.

It is a question that those who love God and the souls of men and women can hardly avoid. With some it is a purely academic question. They would like to solve the question for intellectual satisfaction. Others, mere busybodies, would pry into the future, like many who are curious to know all about the affairs of their neighbors, that they may have something about which to gossip. It is not a matter of vital interest to them. Indeed, they are of that large class of people who have no vital interest in anything. They are like the lying woman in Solomon's day who stole another woman's baby, but had so little real interest in the baby that she was willing to have it cut in two rather than to acknowledge her theft and lie.

With others it is a painfully practical question. Their hearts are in The Salvation Army. It is as dear to them as life. They are bound up in the bundle of its life. They have sacrificed every other interest for it. They are given over to it soul and body, and have dedicated not only themselves, but also their children to it. They feel that the highest interests of the kingdom of God upon earth are bound up with the Army, and the coming and establishment of the kingdom are in large measure dependent upon its spiritual life and prosperity.

There are some people who are sure they know the answer. There are optimists who see nothing but the rosiest future for the Army. But there are pessimists who prophesy its imminent disruption and dissolution.

Many years ago, just after a tour that had taken me around the world, an old officer asked me with a quizzical look, "Are you going to leave the Army ship before she sinks?" I assured him that from a rather wide range of intimate observation I saw no signs that the ship was seriously leaking, or likely to sink, but that even if I did, as an officer my business was to stick to the ship and do all in my power to save it, or go down with it and its precious freightage of the souls of men and women and little children. "A hired hand will run when he sees a wolf coming. . . . The good shepherd sacrifices his life for the sheep" (John 10:12, 11 NLT). And the true officer gives his or her life for The Salvation Army and the souls who are in its keeping.

Doubters and timid souls have been prophesying the end of The Salvation Army from its very beginning, but still it lives and prospers. But what will be its future? Will it continue to live and prosper? Or has it fulfilled its mission?

Like a great bridge hung upon two buttresses, so the Army is buttressed upon God and humanity.

Is it God's Army? Did He inspire and gird and guide William Booth when, with his heart aching for sinful souls and his spirit aflame for the glory of God and the honor of Christ, he stepped out on Mile End Waste and began the work that has developed into The Salvation Army? Is God for us, or against us, or indifferent to us? I can sing for myself,

His love in time past forbids me to think,
He'll leave me at last in trouble to sink;
Each sweet Ebenezer I have in review
Confirms His good pleasure to see me quite through.[2]

But can I be so confident for the Army? His guidance, His overruling providence, His gracious and mighty deliverances in the past are unmistakable. They are on record, known and read by all who care to read. He has overshadowed The Salvation Army with a pillar of cloud and fire as surely as He did ancient Israel. He has gone before and opened the two leaved gates of brass as He did for Cyrus (see Isa. 45:1) and empowered Army officers and soldiers and made them more than conquerors, as He did the apostles and saints of the early church. But do all these wonders of His favor and grace give assurance for the future? Is The Salvation Army sacrosanct? Are we favorites and pets of the Almighty? This leads us to the second point of dependence.

If God is for us, and I fully believe He is, does not that ensure our future? The future of The Salvation Army depends not only upon God—I say it reverently—but also upon you and me and all who have anything to do with the Army. The prophet Azariah cried out, "Hear me, Asa, and all Judah and Benjamin. The LORD is with you while you are with Him. If you seek Him, He will be found by you"—and here is warning for us to heed, for here lurks danger—"but if you forsake Him, He will forsake you" (2 Chron. 15:2 NKJV). And this is a timeless prophecy, eternally true, and not of private interpretation. It is as true today as it was three millennia ago, as true of the Army—of you and of me—as it was of ancient Judah and Benjamin and their king Asa. And it is "written for our admonition, upon whom the ends of the world are come" (1 Cor. 10:11 KJV). Let us search our hearts, order our lives, and be admonished.

Insofar as we have sought God with our whole heart, walked in His ways, and lived and worked in the spirit of our Lord and Master in the past, He has been with us, preserved us, prospered the work of our hands, fulfilled the desires of our hearts, and blessed us in the presence of our enemies. Can we still confidently expect His favor for the future? Yes, but only if we continue to abide in Him and fulfill the conditions that have permitted Him to pour benedictions upon us in the past.

And what are these conditions? I think we shall find them expressed in the closing ministry of Jesus and of Paul. They were expressed by our Lord in those closing days of His ministry when preparing His disciples for His departure and for the days when they must stand alone without His incarnate presence and lay the foundations, build the church, and give it the living example and word that would guide it through the storm and stress of agonizing pagan persecutions, of worldly allurements and seductions, of subtle philosophizings, of pain and poverty, of indifference and scorn, and of the dangers of wealth and power and wide acclaim. And they were expressed through Paul in his later ministry, in his farewell address to the elders of Ephesus at Miletus and in his prison letters to the churches and his young friends and lieutenants, Timothy and Titus.

The warnings, exhortations, example, and the close and intimate instructions of our Lord to His disciples in the closing moments of His ministry, and His High Priestly Prayer recorded in the seventeenth chapter of John, show us the plain path in which we must walk, if the future of The Salvation Army is to be happy and prosperous and its great promise come to ample fulfillment.

And what were the example and teachings of the Master in those fleet, closing days? As He drew near the cross His disciples thought

He was drawing near to a throne and crown, and they were each ambitious and contentious for first place and highest honors. But He told them plainly that He would be rejected and crucified. Then Peter rebuked Him, "Heaven forbid, Lord. . . . This will never happen to you!" (Matt. 16:22 NLT).

But He rebuked Peter and replied, "If any of you wants to be my follower, you must turn from your selfish ways, take up your cross, and follow me" (Matt. 16:24 NLT).

It was not an unusual sight in the Roman Empire to see a line of men following a leader, each bearing a cross on his way to crucifixion. This was the picture He would have them visualize. They were to follow Him, their Leader, each bearing his own cross, not seeking to save his life, but ready to lose it for His sake and for the sake of others. For "all who want to save their lives will lose them. But all who lose their lives because of me will save them" (Luke 9:24 CEB).

So mightily at last did this teaching grip the early disciples and fire their spirits that they actually coveted martyrdom and ran upon death with joy. In this they may have swung to an extreme, but if The Salvation Army of the future is to prosper and win spiritual triumphs, we must follow the Master, not seeking first place or power, but glorying in the cross.

This was Paul's secret. He was the pattern disciple. He had sat at the feet of Jesus and learned of Him until he could write, "What things were gain to me, those I counted loss for Christ" (Phil. 3:7 KJV); "Neither count I my life dear unto myself, so that I might finish my course with joy, and the ministry, which I have received of the Lord Jesus" (Acts 20:24 KJV); "God forbid that I should glory, save in the cross of our Lord Jesus Christ, by whom the world is crucified unto me, and I unto the world" (Gal. 6:14 KJV).

If the future of The Salvation Army is to be spiritually radiant and all-conquering, we must not simply endure the cross, but glory in it. This will arrest the world, disarm hell, and gladden our Lord's heart.

We must "by love serve one another" (Gal. 5:13 KJV). We are following Him who "came not to be ministered unto, but to minister, and to give his life a ransom for many" (Mark 10:45 KJV). We, too, must give our lives for others, shrinking from no service, holding ourselves ever ready to wash the feet of the lowliest disciple.

We must still prove our discipleship by our love for one another. It is not enough to wear the uniform, to profess loyalty to Army leaders and principles, to give our goods to feed the poor and our bodies to be burned. We must love one another. We must make this the badge of our discipleship. We must wrestle and pray and hold fast that we do not lose this.

The Salvation Army is so thoroughly organized and disciplined, so wrought into the life of nations, so fortified with valuable properties, and on such a sound financial basis, that it is not likely to perish as an organization. But it will become a spiritually dead thing if love leaks out. Love is the life of the Army. "If we love one another, God lives in us and his love is made complete in us" (1 John 4:12 NIV). But if love leaks out we shall lose our crown; we shall have a name to live and yet be dead. We may still house the homeless, dole out food to the hungry, punctiliously perform our routine work, but the mighty ministry of the Spirit will no longer be our glory. Our musicians will play meticulously and our singing groups will revel in the artistry of song that tickles the ear but leaves the heart cold and hard. Our officers will hobnob with mayors and council members and be greeted in the marketplace, but God will not be among us. We shall still recruit our ranks and supply our training schools with cadets from among our own young people, but we shall cease to be saviors of the lost sheep that have no shepherd.

If the future of The Salvation Army is to still be glorious, we must heed the exhortation, "Let brotherly love continue" (Heb. 13:1 KJV). We must remember that we are all brothers and sisters and be careful that through leakage of love we do not become like the wicked of whom the psalmist wrote, "You sit and speak against your brother; you slander your own mother's son" (Ps. 50:20 ESV), and find our hearts full of strife and bitter envying where the love that suffers long and is kind should reign supreme.

This is that for which Jesus pleaded on that last night before His crucifixion: "My command is this: Love each other as I have loved you. Greater love has no one than this: to lay down one's life for one's friends. You are my friends if you do what I command. . . . This is my command: Love each other" (John 15:12–14, 17 NIV).

This is that for which Paul pleaded and labored: "May the Lord make your love increase and overflow for each other and for everyone else, just as ours does for you. May he strengthen your hearts so that you will be blameless and holy in the presence of our God and Father when our Lord Jesus comes with all his holy ones" (1 Thess. 3:12–13 NIV).

This is that to which Peter exhorted the universal church: "Now that you have purified yourselves by obeying the truth so that you have sincere love for each other, love one another deeply, from the heart. . . . Above all, love each other deeply, because love covers over a multitude of sins" (1 Pet. 1:22; 4:8 NIV).

How else but by fullness of love for one another can we fulfill those supernatural requirements expressed by Paul and Peter? For more than forty years I have pondered and prayed over those two brief and searching words of Paul: "Be devoted to one another in love. Honor one another above yourselves" (Rom. 12:10 NIV). "Do nothing out of selfish ambition or vain conceit. Rather, in humility value others above yourselves" (Phil. 2:3 NIV).

These are lofty spiritual heights scaled only by those in whose pure hearts burns selfless love. This is the lifeblood—the pulsing, eager, satisfying and yet ever unsatisfied, outreaching, world-embracing lifeblood—of The Salvation Army.

Nothing will so certainly ensure the prosperous and happy future of the Army as this spirit, and I am persuaded that nothing other than this can ensure it. Insofar as this spirit rules in our hearts, God can work with us and bless us, and the spiritual triumphs and glory of the Army for the future are assured. But insofar as these graces of the Spirit in us fail, so far will The Salvation Army as a spiritual power in the earth fail. Organization and government are important, vastly important, for the direction and conservation of our activities, but without the lifeblood the organization is a bit of mere mechanism and the government is a pantomime.

Finally, in closing, let me recommend, for prayerful study and meditation, Paul's farewell address to the elders of Ephesus at Miletus, recorded in Acts 20:17–35. Over and over again and again, through more than four decades, I have read and pondered that address, and prayed that the spirit that was in Paul might be in me and in all my comrades, for this is the spirit of Jesus. This is that for which He prayed on that last night of His agony as recorded in the seventeenth chapter of John. And this is that, and that alone, which can and will ensure the victorious and happy future of our worldwide Salvation Army.

## *NOTES*

1. This question was particularly pertinent in the years following the death of The Salvation Army's founder, William Booth, in 1912. *Ancient Prophets and Modern Problems* was first published in 1929, a year of great transition for the organization, which saw the election of Edward Higgins as the Army's third general and the death of the Army's second general (and William Booth's eldest son), Bramwell.

2. John Newton, "Begone Unbelief," 1779, public domain.

# Samuel L. Brengle's Holy Life Series

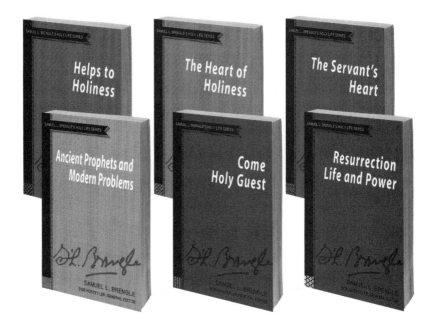

This series comprises the complete works of Samuel L. Brengle, combining all nine of his original books into six volumes, penned by one of the great minds on holiness. Each volume has been lovingly edited for modern readership by popular author (and long-time Brengle devotee) Bob Hostetler. Brengle's authentic voice remains strong, now able to more relevantly engage today's disciples of holiness. These books are must-haves for all who would seriously pursue and understand the depths of holiness in the tradition of John Wesley.

**Helps to Holiness**
ISBN: 978-1-63257-064-2
eBook: 978-1-63257-065-9

**The Heart of Holiness**
ISBN: 978-1-63257-066-6
eBook: 978-1-63257-067-3

**The Servant's Heart**
ISBN: 978-1-63257-068-0
eBook: 978-1-63257-069-7

**Ancient Prophets and Modern Problems**
ISBN: 978-1-63257-070-3
eBook: 978-1-63257-071-0

**Come Holy Guest**
ISBN: 978-1-63257-072-7
eBook: 978-1-63257-073-4

**Resurrection Life and Power**
ISBN: 978-1-63257-074-1
eBook: 978-1-63257-075-8

**Samuel L. Brengle's**
**Holy Life Series Box Set**
ISBN: 978-1-63257-076-5